T·H·E
Authoritative
CALVIN AND HOBBES

Andrews McMeel Publishing®

Kansas City • Sydney • London

Andrews McMeel Publishing, LLC
an Andrews McMeel Universal company
1130 Walnut Street, Kansas City, Missouri 64106

www.andrewsmcmeel.com

ISBN: 978-1-4494-3705-3

Library of Congress Control Number: 90-82675

15 16 17 18 19 SDB 10 9 8 7 6 5 4 3

ATTENTION: SCHOOLS AND BUSINESSES
Andrews McMeel books are available at quantity discounts with bulk purchase for educational, business, or sales promotional use. For information, please e-mail the Andrews McMeel Special Sales Department: specialsales@amuniversal.com.

To Doctor Dave and
Fellow Moosers John, Brad, and The Frey

calvin and HObbES

by WATTERSON

ARRGH! I'M **NEVER** GOING TO BE ABLE TO MEMORIZE ALL THESE DUMB VOCABULARY WORDS!

TRANSMOG-RIFIER

ZAP

TRANSMOG-RIFIER

WUMP WUMP WUMP

HOW CAN ONE LITTLE KID MAKE SO MUCH NOISE?

CALVIN, WHAT ARE YOU DOING UP THERE?! YOU SOUND LIKE AN ELEPHANT! YOU'RE SUPPOSED TO BE DOING YOUR HOMEWORK!

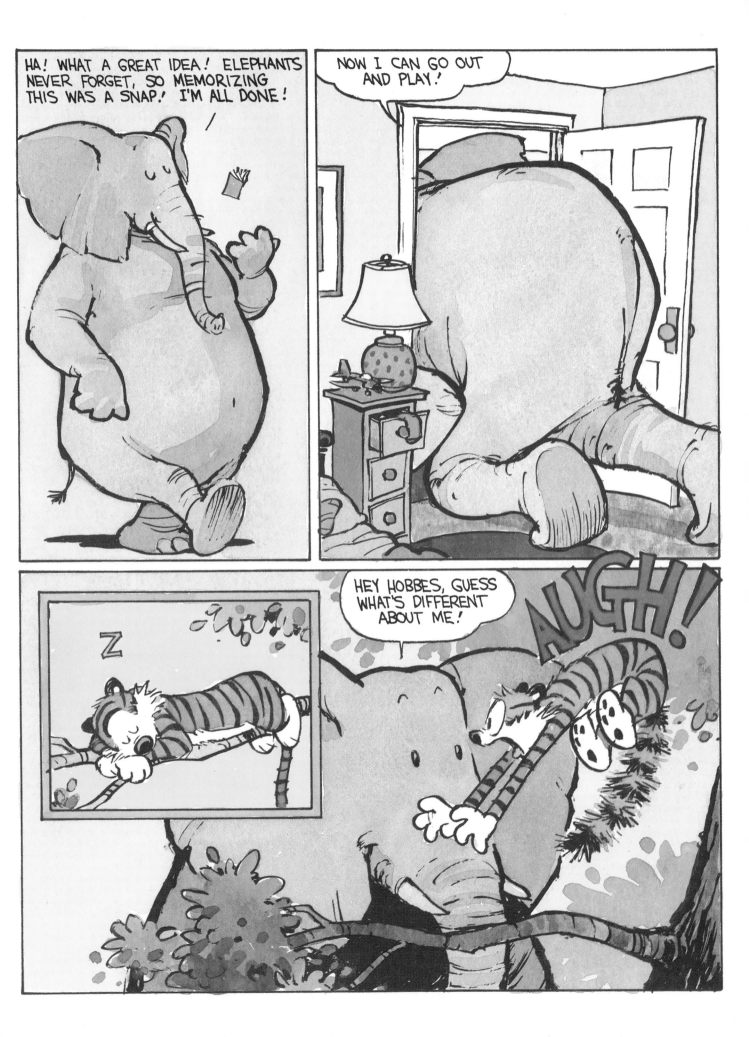

The End.

CalViN and HobbEs

by WATTERSON

"BEFORE BEGINNING ANY HOME-PLUMBING REPAIR, MAKE SURE YOU POSSESS THE PROPER TOOLS FOR THE JOB."

"CHECK THE FOLLOWING LIST OF HANDY EXPLETIVES, AND SEE THAT YOU KNOW HOW TO USE THEM."

CALVIN WAKES UP ONE MORNING TO FIND HE NO LONGER EXISTS IN THE THIRD DIMENSION! HE IS **2-D**!

THINNER THAN A SHEET OF PAPER, CALVIN HAS NO SURFACE AREA ON THE BOTTOM OF HIS FEET! HE IS IMMOBILE!

ONLY BY "WAVING" HIS BODY CAN CALVIN CREATE ENOUGH FRICTION WITH THE GROUND TO MOVE!

HAVING WIDTH BUT NO THICKNESS, CALVIN IS VULNERABLE TO THE SLIGHTEST GUST OF WIND!

TO AVOID DRAFTS, HE TWISTS HIMSELF INTO A TUBE, AND ROLLS ACROSS THE FLOOR!

SOMEONE IS COMING! CALVIN QUICKLY STANDS UP STRAIGHT.

TURNING PERFECTLY SIDEWAYS, HE IS A NEARLY INVISIBLE VERTICAL LINE! NO ONE WILL NOTICE!

HEY DAD, KNOW WHY YOU DIDN'T SEE ME ALL MORNING?? I WAS TWO-DIMENSIONAL!

HMMM, I'LL BET YOU CAN'T DO IT ALL AFTERNOON, TOO...

DEAR!

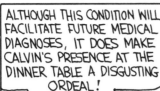
BOMBARDED BY HIGH-ENERGY PHOTONS, CALVIN IS TRANSFORMED INTO A LIVING X-RAY!

ALTHOUGH THIS CONDITION WILL FACILITATE FUTURE MEDICAL DIAGNOSES, IT DOES MAKE CALVIN'S PRESENCE AT THE DINNER TABLE A DISGUSTING ORDEAL!

EVERYONE CAN SEE CALVIN'S FOOD BEING GROUND INTO MUSHY PULP AND SWALLOWED! AT THIS MOMENT, CALVIN CHEWS UP A LARGE SPOONFUL OF CREAMED CORN!

FOR GOSH SAKES, CLOSE YOUR MOUTH WHEN YOU CHEW!! YOU THINK WE WANT TO *SEE* THAT?!

MKGHH! SMACK! BLAGHKH!

HERE'S A LITTLE TOWN.

HERE'S A STEAMSHOVEL SCOOPING OUT A GIANT HOLE.

HERE COMES THE BULLDOZER, PUSHING THOUSANDS OF BARRELS OF TOXIC NUCLEAR WASTE INTO THE GIANT HOLE.

OVER THE YEARS, THESE DANGEROUS POISONS SEEP INTO UNDERGROUND WATERWAYS.

THE CANCER RATE OF THE NEARBY LITTLE TOWN TRIPLES.

IF YOU WANT ME, I'LL BE UNDER THE BED.

A STRIKE?!? THAT PITCH WAS FOUR FEET ABOVE MY HEAD!

HA! IT WAS A *PERFECT* PITCH! YOU'RE JUST TOO SHORT!

YEAH? WELL, *YOU'RE* JUST TOO STUPID!

WELL, YOU'RE JUST TOO *UGLY!*

KICK KICK KICK KICK

KICKING DUST IS THE ONLY PART OF THIS GAME WE REALLY LIKE.

CaLViN and HObbEs
by WATTERSON

I'M GOING OUTSIDE, MOM!

HOLD ALL MY CALLS.

CALVIN LOOKS AROUND. SOMETHING IS DIFFERENT.

THE ODD-COLORED TREE BEHIND HIM SLOWLY LIFTS UP! IT'S NOT A TREE AT ALL! IT'S A LEG!

OH NO! CALVIN IS THE SIZE OF A BUG *TO* A BUG! HE RUNS FOR HIS LIFE!

A CLAW CRASHES WITH DEAFENING IMPACT! THE BUG IS TRYING TO STEP ON CALVIN! WHAT A HORRIBLE FATE!

CALVIN SCRAMBLES MADLY, PROMISING HIMSELF THAT HE'LL NEVER SQUISH ANOTHER BUG IF HE LIVES TO RETURN TO NORMAL SIZE!

SUDDENLY IN A SPRAY OF SLIME, THE BUG IS GONE! A MONSTROUS FROG LICKS ITS CHOPS! CALVIN IS SAVED!

AACCK! WHAT'S THAT ON MY PLATE?! GOOD HEAVENS, GET IT OFF THE TABLE!!

BUT MOM, FROGS ARE OUR *FRIENDS*!

OH BOY OH BOY OH BOY OH BOY OH BOY OH BOY OH BOY OH BOY OH BOY OH BOY

WAIT! WAIT! I'VE GOT TO SAVOR THIS MOMENT! THE BRILLIANCE OF IT ALL! I'M A GENIUS! A SHEER *GENIUS!*

SUSIE'S PLAYING ON THE SIDEWALK! NOW'S MY CHANCE TO USE THE SNOWBALL I'VE BEEN SAVING IN THE FREEZER!

SHE'LL NEVER EXPECT A SNOWBALL IN *JUNE!* BOY, WILL SHE BE MAD! HA HA HA!

THIS IS GOING TO BE GREAT! HERE IT COMES! OH BOY! OH BOY!

HEY SUSIE!!

PIFF

I *MISSED!* DARN IT DARN IT DARN IT!! OF ALL THE MISERABLE LUCK!

AAARRGHH!

THERE MUST'VE BEEN A CROSS BREEZE! I CAN'T BELIEVE IT! I SAVED THAT SNOWBALL FOR THREE WHOLE MONTHS! I...

SCOOP SCOOP

I.. I...UH...

POW

THE IRONY OF THIS IS JUST SICKENING.

"1988 ISN'T TOO FAR AWAY, DAD."

"IF YOU'RE THINKING OF RUNNING FOR "DAD" AGAIN, YOU'D BETTER GET YOUR CAMPAIGN IN GEAR."

"FRANKLY, THE POLLS LOOK GRIM. I DON'T THINK YOU'VE GOT MUCH OF A SHOT AT KEEPING THE OFFICE."

"I TAKE COMFORT IN THE FACT THAT NOT MANY PEOPLE WOULD WANT IT."

"FLIPPANT REMARKS HAVE A WAY OF HAUNTING CANDIDATES, YOU KNOW."

"THE CHAMELEON SITS MOTIONLESS."

"AMAZINGLY, THE LIZARD CHANGES COLOR TO BLEND IN WITH HIS SURROUNDINGS."

"MOMENTS LATER, HE IS VIRTUALLY INVISIBLE."

"I SEE YOU HIDING BACK THERE! NOW COME CLEAN UP THIS MESS YOU MADE IN THE KITCHEN!"

"HOLD STILL. THERE'S A MONSTER HORSEFLY ON YOUR HEAD."

POW!!

"CAN YOU BELIEVE IT? I MISSED!"

!

"SO EXCUSE ME FOR TRYING TO HELP! YOU WANNA SCRATCH A STINGING WELT ALL DAY? FINE! GO AWAY!"

"NO, WAIT. THERE'S A MOSQUITO ON YOU."

31

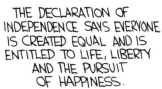

CALVIN AND HOBBES by WATTERSON

THE DREADED SCUM BEINGS FIRE! SPACEMAN SPIFF IS *HIT!*

IT NEVER FAILS. I JUST WASHED AND WAXED THIS THING.

OUR HERO, THE INTREPID SPACEMAN SPIFF, STRUGGLES WITH THE CONTROLS OF HIS DAMAGED SPACECRAFT!

THE FREEM PROPULSION BLASTERS ARE USELESS! SPIFF CRASHES ONTO THE SURFACE OF AN ALIEN PLANET!

UNSCATHED, THE FEARLESS SPACE EXPLORER EMERGES FROM THE SMOLDERING WRECKAGE! HE IS MAROONED ON A HOSTILE WORLD!

SCORCHED BY TWIN SUNS, THE PLANET IS NOTHING BUT BARREN ROCK AND METHANE! THERE'S NO HOPE OF FINDING FOOD OR WATER!

SPIFF COLLAPSES! OH NO, A HIDEOUS ALIEN SPOTS HIM! IN HIS WEAKENED STATE, SPIFF IS NO MATCH FOR THE MONSTER! *THIS COULD BE THE END!!*

LUNCHTIME! I BROUGHT YOU A SANDWICH AND SOME LEMONADE.

BRING THE DISHES BACK WHEN YOU'RE DONE, OK?

...OH WELL.

THANKS, MOM.

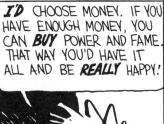

AREN'T THESE LONG SUMMER DAYS GREAT? NO RESPONSIBILITIES AT ALL! WE HAVE THE WHOLE DAY TO OURSELVES.

DON'T YOU WISH IT COULD BE LIKE THIS ALL YEAR, FOREVER? NO SCHOOL, NO JOB, NO ANYTHING?

YEAH, JUST GLOAT ABOUT IT, WHY DON'T YOU!!

HEY DAD, WHAT ARE CLOUDS MADE OF?

HMM... I USED TO KNOW THAT. I THINK THEY'RE MOSTLY WATER.

SO HOW COME THEY FLOAT?

WELL, IT'S SORT OF EVAPORATED WATER. MAYBE THERE ARE SOME OTHER GASES, TOO. I'M NOT SURE.

SO WHY ARE THEY WHITE WHEN THE REST OF THE SKY IS BLUE?

HECK, BEATS ME. I GUESS WE OUGHT TO LOOK THIS STUFF UP.

I TAKE IT THERE'S NO QUALIFYING EXAM TO BE A DAD.

ONE OF THE BEST THINGS ABOUT SUMMER IS GOING TO SLEEP WITH THE FAN ON.

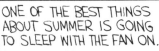

THE GENTLE BREEZE BLOWING, THE DRONING HUM...EVERYTHING SEEMS SAFE AND SERENE WHEN THE FAN IS ON.

IT'S COOL AND LULLING AND PERFECT FOR SLEEP.

IT ALMOST LETS ONE FORGET HE HAS A HEAVY FUR COAT FOR A BUNKMATE.

IF YOU DON'T LIKE IT, THERE'S PLENTY OF ROOM ON THE FLOOR, BUSTER.

HEY MOM, WHAT'S THIS I HEAR ABOUT THE GREENHOUSE EFFECT?

THEY SAY THE POLLUTANTS WE DUMP IN THE AIR ARE TRAPPING IN THE SUN'S HEAT AND IT'S GOING TO MELT THE POLAR ICE CAPS!

SURE, *YOU'LL* BE GONE WHEN IT HAPPENS, BUT *I* WON'T! NICE PLANET YOU'RE LEAVING ME!

THIS FROM THE KID WHO WANTS TO BE CHAUFFEURED ANY PLACE MORE THAN A BLOCK AWAY.

HEY, NOBODY TOLD ME ABOUT THE ICE CAPS, ALL RIGHT?

MORE BAD NEWS ON YOUR POLLS, DAD. WE'RE LOOKING AT AN ALL-TIME LOW IN POPULARITY HERE.

WELL, CALVIN, THAT'S CERTAINLY FOOD FOR THOUGHT.

NOW HERE'S SOMETHING *YOU* CAN THINK ABOUT. THE AVERAGE COST OF RAISING A KID TO AGE 18 IS $100,000. THAT'S A LOT OF MONEY.

SO THE QUESTION YOU SHOULD BE ASKING YOURSELF IS, "IS THAT HUNDRED GRAND A **GIFT**... OR A **LOAN**?"

GOTCHA, DAD. I WAS JUST ON MY WAY TO BED.

RING RING

HELLO?

MAY I SPEAK WITH YOUR FATHER, PLEASE?

HECK, YOU DON'T NEED *MY* PERMISSION! BE MY GUEST!

WHAT A WEIRDO.

RING RING

I CAN'T BELIEVE HOW DULL MY LIFE IS. IT'S SO BORING HERE.

NOTHING EVER CHANGES AROUND HERE. NOTHING EVER HAPPENS.

IT SEEMS AS IF (HANG ON) EVERYBODY BUT ME GETS TO HAVE AN EXCITING LIFE.

ACTUALLY, I'D LIKE *LESS* EXCITEMENT IN MY LIFE.

WHY? ARE YOU DOING FUN THINGS WHEN I'M NOT AROUND?? HUH? *ARE* YOU?!

WHAT'S WRONG, CALVIN? WHY ARE YOU STILL IN BED?

I DON'T FEEL GOOD.

YOUR FOREHEAD SEEMS WARM. WE'D BETTER TAKE YOUR TEMPERATURE.

I CAN'T BE SICK *NOW!* IT'S STILL SUMMER VACATION! THERE'S NO SCHOOL TO STAY HOME FROM! THIS IS *MY* TIME!

SOMEBODY OWES ME BIG FOR THIS!!

HI THERE, CALVIN. I UNDERSTAND YOU'RE NOT FEELING WELL.

ME? I'M FINE! I JUST SIT AROUND TORTURE CHAMBERS IN MY UNDERWEAR FOR KICKS. LET'S SEE YOUR DEGREE, YOU QUACK!

I'M NOT GOING TO HURT YOU. I'M JUST GOING TO EXAMINE YOU TO SEE WHAT'S WRONG.

I'LL TELL YOU WHAT'S WRONG! I'VE GOT DR. FRANKENSTEIN FOR A PEDIATRICIAN, *THAT'S* WHAT'S WRONG!

NURSE, CALL THE ANESTHESIOLOGIST IN HERE, WILL YOU PLEASE?

MY DAD'S A LAWYER, I'LL HAVE YOU KNOW! DON'T COME NEAR ME!

DEEP IN A DANK DUNGEON ON THE DISMAL PLANET ZOG, THE FEARLESS SPACEMAN SPIFF IS HELD PRISONER BY THE SINISTER ZOG KING.

A GUARD LEADS SPIFF TO THE INTERROGATION ROOM. OUR HERO IS STOIC AND DEFIANT!

AT LAST I MEET THE FAMED SPACEMAN SPIFF! I TRUST YOU ARE...HEH HEH... ENJOYING YOUR VISIT?

YOU'RE WASTING YOUR TIME, MAGGOT FROM MARS! I'LL NEVER GIVE IN!

NEVER, YOU HEAR ME?! *NEVER!*

KID, DON'T MAKE ME RECANT THE HIPPOCRATIC OATH, OK?

WELL, YOU CERTAINLY WERE A TERROR IN THE DOCTOR'S OFFICE.

I FENDED HIM OFF WITH HIS OWN TONGUE DEPRESSOR. THAT'S WHY I DIDN'T GET A SHOT.

YOU DIDN'T *NEED* A SHOT. YOUR BEHAVIOR WAS INEXCUSABLE.

ALL THAT COUNTS IS THAT HE COULDN'T GET NEAR ENOUGH TO STICK ME. HE THINKS I'M A LITTLE PINK PIN CUSHION IN UNDERPANTS.

SOMEDAY I HOPE YOU HAVE A KID THAT PUTS YOU THROUGH WHAT I'VE GONE THROUGH.

YEAH, GRANDMA SAYS THAT'S WHAT SHE USED TO TELL *YOU.*

HERE IS A PROUD CITY, FULL OF HAPPY, PROSPEROUS CITIZENS.

THEY GO ON ABOUT THEIR BUSINESS, **UNAWARE** THAT THE MOON HAS MYSTERIOUSLY MOVED A FEW MILES CLOSER TO THE EARTH.

...UNAWARE, THAT IS, UNTIL THE TIDE COMES IN.

SPLOOSH!

GISSHHH!

44

Calvin and Hobbes
by WATTERSON

THE FIRE'S NOT LIGHTING, HUH? CAN I MAKE A SUGGESTION?

GIVE UP ON THAT SISSY LIGHTER FLUID.

CAN'T WE COOK THE HAMBURGERS YET?

THE COALS AREN'T HOT ENOUGH.

BUT I'M HUNGRY! I WANT TO EAT *NOW!*

WELL, YOU'LL JUST HAVE TO WAIT.

YOU KNOW, CALVIN, SOMETIMES THE ANTICIPATION OF SOMETHING IS MORE FUN THAN THE THING ITSELF ONCE YOU GET IT.

HERE WE ARE, IT'S A BEAUTIFUL EVENING. IT'S NICE TO JUST SIT HERE AND LOOK AT THE TREES WHILE WE WAIT FOR THE COALS TO GET HOT, DON'T YOU THINK?

DINNER WILL BE OVER SOON, AND AFTERWARD WE'LL BE DISTRACTED WITH OTHER THINGS TO DO. BUT NOW WE HAVE A FEW MINUTES TO OURSELVES TO ENJOY THE EVENING.

THESE SUMMER DAYS GO BY SO QUICKLY. IT'S GOOD THAT EVERY NOW AND THEN WE HAVE TO WAIT FOR SOMETHING.

SO SHOULD I GO TO McDONALD'S THEN, OR WHAT?

YEAH, I KNOW. YOU THINK YOU'RE GOING TO BE SIX ALL YOUR LIFE.

WHAT A PERFECT DAY!

ISN'T IT GREAT TO BE ON SUMMER VACATION? TO BE ABLE TO ENJOY ALL THIS WITH NO SCHOOL AND NO RESPONSIBILITIES?

..AHHHHHHHH...

I CAN'T BELIEVE THERE'S NOTHING ON TV BUT REPEATS.

I THINK A BEE LANDED ON MY BACK! CAN YOU SEE IT? I DON'T WANT TO MOVE!

THAT'S NOT A BEE.

IT ISN'T? *WHEW*

NO, THAT'S A HORNET IF I EVER SAW ONE!

OW!

46

Calvin and Hobbes

by Watterson

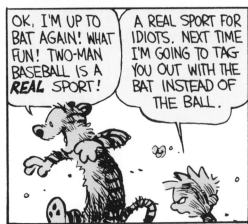

WHEN'S THIS RAIN GOING TO LET UP?

I DON'T KNOW, CALVIN.

HEY, CHEER UP, GANG! I PACKED STORM GEAR. "ALWAYS BE PREPARED," YOU KNOW.

THESE PONCHOS ARE SUPER. THEY'RE THERMAL-SEALED LIGHTWEIGHT NYLON, LAMINATED WITH FLEXIBLE URETHANE FOR COMPLETE WATER PROTECTION!

YEAH, DAD. IT'S GREAT THAT WE WON'T GET WETTER THAN WE ALREADY ARE.

ZINC OXIDE, THONGS, TANNING LOTION... WRONG DUFFEL BAG. LET'S SEE, WHICH ONE OF THESE WAS IT?

I'M GLAD DAD FINALLY GOT THE TENTS UP. NOW I CAN GET OUT OF THESE SOGGY CLOTHES.

TOO BAD *YOU* CAN'T PUT ON DRY CLOTHES. YOU'D FEEL A LOT BETTER.

HEY, WAIT! **NO!** **DON'T DO THAT HERE!!**

ACKPTH!

SOME TROUPER *YOU* ARE! WHAT'S A LITTLE RAIN? THIS IS WHAT BEING IN THE WILDERNESS IS ALL ABOUT!

HA HA! AT LEAST IT'S NOT *SNOWING*, RIGHT?

RIGHT?

I MEAN, SAY IT WAS SNOWING SO HARD WE COULDN'T MAKE A FIRE.

BOY, I LOVE COLD CANNED RAVIOLI.

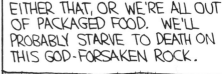

WELL, GANG, I'M SORRY THE WEATHER WASN'T ANY BETTER THIS WEEK.

I KNOW IT WASN'T ALWAYS A LOT OF FUN, BUT WE LIVED THROUGH IT, AND WE GOT TO SPEND SOME TIME TOGETHER, AND THAT'S WHAT'S REALLY IMPORTANT.

ANYWAY, I HOPE YOU'RE ALL NOT *TOO* DISAPPOINTED.

CALVIN, TELL YOUR DAD ANY JUDGE WOULD TAKE THIS TRIP AS GROUNDS FOR DIVORCE.

DAD, MOM SAYS...

ALL RIGHT! ALL RIGHT!

DAD, CAN YOU GET MY BALL OUT OF THE GUTTER AGAIN?

THIS IS THE THIRD TIME THIS AFTERNOON! I THOUGHT I TOLD YOU TO PLAY OUT BACK!

RELAX, DAD. IT'S JUST A BALL IN THE GUTTER. IT'S NOT AS IF I'VE BEEN EMBEZZLING MONEY OR KILLING PEOPLE, RIGHT? AREN'T YOU GLAD I'M NOT STEALING AND MURDERING?

I ALWAYS HAVE TO HELP DAD ESTABLISH THE PROPER CONTEXT.

C'MON, HOBBES. LET DOWN THE ROPE LADDER.

WHAT'S THE REST OF THE PASSWORD?

I THINK FIVE VERSES EXTOLLING TIGERS IS *PLENTY*. YOU KNOW IT'S ME! LET ME UP!

NO.

OOH, WHY YOU LOUSY, ROTTEN, STINKING..

IF YOU CALL ME NAMES, YOU HAVE TO START OVER AT THE BEGINNING.

VERSE SIX: "TIGERS ARE NIMBLE AND LIGHT ON THEIR TOES, MY *RE*SPECT FOR TIGERS CONTINUALLY GROWS."

YOU'RE NOT DOING THE DANCE.

Calvin and Hobbes by WATTERSON

AH·CHOO!

WHEW ... NO BRAINS.

AH.. AH.. AH.. AH

CHOOO!!

THE FORCE OF THE NASAL EXPLOSION SENDS CALVIN REELING THROUGH THE STRATOSPHERE!

WITH LESS AND LESS AIR TO RESIST HIS MOMENTUM, HE BREAKS THE PULL OF EARTH'S GRAVITY AND HURLS PAST THE MOON!

AS HE PASSES OUT OF THE GALAXY, CALVIN REFLECTS ON THE WISDOM OF COVERING ONE'S MOUTH WHEN SNEEZING TO DEFLECT THE PROPULSION.

ALAS, IT IS KNOWLEDGE GAINED TOO LATE FOR POOR CALVIN, THE HUMAN SATELLITE! ...BUT WAIT! ANOTHER SNEEZE IS BREWING! CALVIN TURNS HIMSELF AROUND!

THE SECOND SNEEZE ROCKETS HIM BACK TO EARTH! HE'S SAVED! IT'S A MIRACLE!

AH CHOO!

GOD BLESS YOU.

OH, HE *DOES*, MOM. HE *DOES*.

WATTERSON

RATS. I CAN'T TELL MY GUM FROM MY SILLY PUTTY.

WAP WAP WAP WAP

WIPPITY WAPPITY WIPPITY WAPPITY

BIPPITABIPPITABIPPITABIPPITABIPPITA

I'M NEVER GONNA GET MARRIED. ARE YOU?

HMM... I SUPPOSE IF THE RIGHT PERSON CAME ALONG, I MIGHT.

SOMEBODY WITH GREEN EYES AND A NICE LAUGH, WHO I COULD CALL "POOTY PIE".

"POOTY PIE"??

OR "BITSY POOKUMS."

I THINK THAT WOULD AFFECT MY STOMACH A LOT MORE THAN MY HEART.

"BITSY POOKUMS," I'D SAY. "YES, SNOOGY WOOGY," SHE'D REPLY...

Calvin and Hobbes
by Watterson

LET'S HAVE A LOOK AROUND. I'M SURE WE'LL RUN INTO A ROBOT OR SOMETHING.

TIME MACHINE

LOOK AT THIS.

GOSH, I WONDER WHAT FUTURISTIC DEVICE THIS IS! SOME SORT OF TRANSPORTATION POD, I'D GUESS.

I WONDER HOW YOU GET IN?

I DON'T SEE A DOOR OR LICENSE NUMBER ANYWHERE.

THIS IS VERY PECULIAR.

HAVE YOU EVER SEEN A TREE THIS COLOR?

I MUST SAY, THE FUTURE IS QUITE A BIT DIFFERENT THAN I EXPECTED.

THIS BREEZE IS SO HOT AND MUGGY. I FIGURED THEY'D BE ABLE TO CONTROL THE WEATHER BY NOW.

THE AIR STINKS, TOO. I GUESS THERE'S STILL POLLUTION.

EVER FEEL AS IF YOU'RE BEING MONITORED?

...OR THAT YOU'RE ABOUT TO DO A DOUBLE-TAKE?

AAUGH BACK TO THE TIME MACHINE! RUN!

WE MUST'VE GONE BACK IN TIME INSTEAD OF FORWARD!

WHAT TIPPED YOU OFF? THE DINOSAUR?!

DON'T GET SMART, FUZZBRAIN. JUST GET IN AND FACE THE OTHER DIRECTION SO WE GO INTO THE FUTURE THIS TIME!

YOU MEAN WE WENT INTO THE PAST BECAUSE WE WERE FACING THE WRONG WAY?!?

YOU THINK I'VE GOT SOME TRIPLE-A MAP?! MAYBE YOU'D LIKE TO STEER THIS TIME!

WE MADE IT! IT'S A GOOD THING THE TIME MACHINE DIDN'T STALL, OR WE'D HAVE BEEN EATEN BY DINOSAURS!

WE'RE COMING BACK TOWARD THE PRESENT NOW. DO YOU WANT TO STOP AT HOME, OR KEEP GOING INTO THE FUTURE LIKE WE PLANNED?

I'VE HAD ENOUGH TIME TRAVELING. LET'S GO HOME.

LET'S GO JUST A *LITTLE* INTO THE FUTURE AND SEE WHAT I'M LIKE AS A TEEN-AGER!

LET'S NOT, ALL RIGHT?

HI, MOM. HOBBES AND I WENT TIME TRAVELING AND VISITED THE JURASSIC PERIOD TODAY.

THAT'S NICE. WHAT'S IT LIKE?

PRETTY SCARY. A DINOSAUR ALMOST ATE US.

ACTUALLY, WE WERE TRYING TO GO INTO THE FUTURE, BUT WE MADE A MISTAKE.

I SEE. WELL, I'M GLAD YOU MADE IT BACK.

YOUR MOM ISN'T FAZED BY MUCH, IS SHE?

IT DEPENDS. SHE DIDN'T TAKE THE FROGS IN THE TOILET SO WELL, REMEMBER?

DAD, LOOK! THE SUN'S SETTING AND IT'S ONLY 3 O'CLOCK!

IT'S NOT 3 O'CLOCK. YOUR WATCH STOPPED.

TIME DOESN'T STOP IF YOUR WATCH STOPS?

NOPE.

PHOOEY. FOR A MOMENT THERE, I THOUGHT I'D GET RICH PATENTING THIS THING.

I'D HAVE BOUGHT ONE.

IF YOU COULD HAVE THREE WISHES GRANTED, WHAT WOULD THEY BE?

JUST THREE WISHES, HUH? HMM... THAT WOULD BE A TOUGH DECISION.

I GUESS I'D HAVE TO THINK ABOUT IT A WHILE.

OOPS! HANG ON.

OK, I KNOW WHAT MY FIRST WISH WOULD BE.

ONE OF NATURE'S UGLIER CREATURES, THE BAT IS A MISUNDERSTOOD MARVEL OF EVOLUTION.

PRODUCING A SERIES OF LOUD, HIGH-PITCHED SQUEAKS, THE BAT CAN JUDGE AN INSECT'S DISTANCE AND ELEVATION BY THE TIME DELAY OF THE SQUEAK'S ECHO!

CHANGES IN THE ECHO'S PITCH REVEAL THE DOOMED BUG'S DIRECTION! NO MOVEMENT ESCAPES THE INCREDIBLE SENSES OF THE BAT!

GLUMP!

TA-DAA! EYES CLOSED!

CALVIN, SIT UP AND EAT WITH A FORK LIKE A CIVILIZED HUMAN BEING.

YAWN

WAAUUGHH!

FOR THE LAST TIME, GET OUT OF BED! WE'RE GOING TO BE LATE.

I'M TRYING. I'M TRYING.

Panel 1: WELL, I GUESS WE'RE ALL PACKED. COMIC BOOKS, DART GUN, SPACE HELMET AND TOBOGGAN! WE'RE OFF TO THE YUKON!

Panel 2: DO WE HAVE A MAP?

OOH, THAT'S RIGHT! GLAD YOU REMEMBERED! I'LL GO GET ONE!

Panel 3: DON'T WE HAVE ANY ROAD MAPS OF THE YUKON, MOM?

I DOUBT IT.

Panel 4: OK, HERE'S THE YUKON. NOW SEE IF YOU CAN FIND THE UNITED STATES.

HERE THEY ARE! LOOK HOW CLOSE IT IS! THIS WON'T TAKE ANY TIME AT ALL!

Panel 5: SO LONG, "MOM"! WE'RE OFF TO THE YUKON. IT'S BEEN NICE LIVING HERE ...BUT NOT *REAL* NICE! HA HA!

Panel 7: CALVIN! WAIT A MINUTE.

LEAVE IT TO A MOTHER TO DRAG OUT A GOODBYE. SHEESH.

Panel 8: YOU'RE GOING SOUTHEAST. NORTH IS *THAT* WAY.

OH YEAH. I KNEW THAT.

Panel 9: THIS SLED IS HEAVY. I THOUGHT WE WERE GOING TO *RIDE* IT MOST OF THE WAY TO THE YUKON.

Panel 10: WE'VE ONLY BEEN WALKING 20 MINUTES, HOBBES. WE PROBABLY WON'T GET TO NORTHERN CANADA UNTIL THIS AFTERNOON.

Panel 11: IN THAT CASE, I'M TAKING A BREAK.

GOOD IDEA. WANT A COMIC BOOK? HERE'S CAPTAIN NITRO.

Panel 12: I WANT A SANDWICH.

WE JUST HAVE ONE APIECE. WE SHOULD SAVE 'EM IN CASE WE CAN'T CATCH A WALRUS.

68

Calvin and Hobbes

by WATTERSON

HOBBES, YOU MANGY FUZZ-BRAINED LUNK HEAD, WHERE ARE YOU?

...I DIDN'T MEAN THAT QUITE THE WAY THAT SOUNDED.

C'MON, CALVIN, GET BACK INSIDE. IT'S TOO LATE TO GO SEARCHING FOR YOUR STUFFED TIGER NOW.

I CAN'T LEAVE HOBBES ALONE IN THE WOODS AT NIGHT!

WELL, MAYBE YOU SHOULD HAVE THOUGHT ABOUT THAT BEFORE IT GOT DARK. THIS CAN BE A LITTLE LESSON, HMM?

I THOUGHT HE'D COME BACK BY HIMSELF. I DIDN'T THINK HE'D GET *LOST!*

WE'LL LOOK FOR HIM TOMORROW. NOW OFF TO BED WITH YOU.

(SNIFF) I HOPE HE'S OK. IF HE HADN'T BEEN ACTING SO STUPID I NEVER WOULD'VE LEFT HIM.

I SURE WISH HE'D COME BACK.

CALVIN LEFT HOBBES SOMEWHERE IN THE WOODS. THE POOR KID'S PRETTY UPSET.

I'LL BET.

I MEAN, HE'S *REALLY* UPSET.

I SAID I'LL BET HE IS.

REALLY UPSET.

..AHH...

WOULD *MY* DAD HAVE DONE THIS? OF COURSE NOT. *I* WAS NEVER SPOILED LIKE THIS...

WATTERSON

69

HI, CALVIN. I BROUGHT MR. BUN OVER SO WE CAN PLAY HOUSE. YOU AND I CAN BE THE PARENTS, AND HOBBES AND MR. BUN CAN BE OUR CHILDREN.

OH, RIGHT. HOBBES AND I ARE GONNA PUT OUR BIG PLANS ON HOLD SO WE CAN PLAY HOUSE WITH A STUFFED RABBIT? FORGET IT!

I DON'T SEE WHY YOU'LL PLAY WITH YOUR DUMB OL' TIGER AND NOT WITH MR. BUN AND ME! YOU'RE JUST MEAN, THAT'S ALL!

GO PLAY IN A MICROWAVE, SUSIE. WE'RE BUSY.

GIRLS ARE LIKE SLUGS— THEY PROBABLY SERVE SOME PURPOSE, BUT IT'S HARD TO IMAGINE WHAT.

MR. BUN SEEMS COMATOSE. DID YOU NOTICE?

HI, DAD. I'M REPEATING EVERYTHING ANYONE SAYS.

OH, YOU ARE, ARE YOU?

OH, YOU ARE, ARE YOU?

KNOCK IT OFF, CALVIN. THAT'S VERY ANNOYING.

KNOCK IT OFF, CALVIN. THAT'S VERY ANNOYING.

I FORFEIT ALL MY DESSERTS FOR A WEEK.

OK, GIVE THEM TO *ME*.

HA HA. WHY DON'T YOU GO BOTHER YOUR MOTHER FOR A WHILE?

WHERE ARE YOU GOING WITH THE TOY TELEPHONE?

OUT IN THE WOODS. YOU CAN COME ALONG IF YOU'D LIKE.

WHAT ARE YOU GOING TO DO?

TRY SOME BIRD CALLS.

CaLViN and HObbEs

by WATTERSON

HA HA! RIGHT HERE, KID!

EEP!

HELP! HELP! THE LEAF PILE'S GOT ME!!

CRUNCH CRUNCH

THE RAKE! GOTTA GET THE RAKE!

FORGET IT, KID! YOU'RE DOOMED!

YAAHH! BACK, YOU ARBOREAL MENACE! BACK!

WHAM WHAM

SINISTER FIEND! YOU WON'T BE TRICKING *OTHER* INNOCENT LITTLE KIDS! I'LL SPREAD YOU ACROSS THE WHOLE YARD!

I THOUGHT YOU SAID YOU WERE GOING TO RAKE THE YARD TODAY.

I *DID* RAKE THE YARD. I SPENT ALL AFTERNOO--

WHERE'S CALVIN?!

CALVIN? ARE YOU IN THERE? C'MON OUT AND WE'LL MAKE SOME POPCORN.

CALVIN? ...OH BROTHER...

I SEE YOU, CALVIN! C'MON BACK INSIDE!

NO WAY, LADY! IF YOU WANT US, YOU'LL HAVE TO *CATCH* US!

OH GEEZ, *RUN!!* SHE'S WEARING *CLEATS!*

OUTTA MY *WAY!* OUTTA MY *WAY!*

LET'S GO! BACK IN THE HOUSE! NO MORE MONKEY BUSINESS, ALL RIGHT?

PHOOEY.

IT'S MY JOB TO WATCH YOU AND THAT'S WHAT I'M GOING TO DO, EVEN IF I HAVE TO STRAP YOU TO A CHAIR.

GOT IT?

JAWOHL, MEIN FÜHRER!

CLIK

CARE TO REPEAT THAT LITTLE COMMENT?

I SAID I'M NOT GOING ANYWHERE. LEGGO.

WE'RE HOME, ROSALYN. WAS CALVIN ANY TROUBLE?

NOT TOO MUCH. I SENT HIM TO BED A LITTLE WHILE AGO.

THAT'S GOOD.

KNOCK KNOCK

NOW WHO COULD THAT BE AT *THIS* HOUR?

POLICE, SIR. WE RECEIVED A CALL ABOUT TWO HOSTAGES BEING HELD HERE.

CALVIN! GET DOWN HERE!!

Calvin and Hobbes

75

UH OH, IT HAPPENED AGAIN.

CALVIN WAKES UP WITHOUT ANY RECOGNIZABLE FEATURES, SAVE TWO ANTENNAE. HOW DISGUSTING.

HE OOZES OUT OF BED ON A TRAIL OF SLIME. LACKING ARMS AND LEGS, HOW WILL CALVIN PUT ON HIS CLOTHES?

AREN'T YOU DRESSED YET? YOU ARE SO SLUGGISH IN THE MORNING!

PSST...SUSIE! WHAT'S THE ANSWER TO QUESTION FOUR?

IMADOOFUS.

THANKS!

THE TOOTH FAIRY'S GONNA MAKE YOU RICH TONIGHT, SUSIE.

LET'S SEE WHAT YOU DREW FOR ART CLASS, SUSIE.

WELL, A TIDY LITTLE DOMESTIC SCENE. A HOUSE IN A YARD WITH FLOWERS. HOW TYPICALLY FEMALE.

GIRLS THINK SMALL AND ARE PREOCCUPIED WITH PETTY DETAILS. BUT *BOYS* THINK *BIG!* BOYS THINK ABOUT ACTION AND ACCOMPLISHMENT! NO WONDER IT'S *MEN* WHO CHANGE THE WORLD!

YEAH? WHAT DID *YOU* DRAW?

A SQUADRON OF B-1s NUKING NEW YORK.

MOM, CAN HOBBES AND I RENT A VCR AND A TAPE TONIGHT?

I DON'T THINK SO, CALVIN. IT'S A SCHOOL NIGHT.

WHAT IF WE GOT AN *EDUCATIONAL* TAPE?

LIKE WHAT?

"CANNIBAL STEWARDESS VIXENS UNCHAINED."

NOW SHE WON'T EVEN LET US GO INTO THE *STORE*.

I THINK WE'D LEARN A *LOT* BY WATCHING THAT.

NOBODY HAD BETTER BE SNEAKING UP ON ME!!

WHUMP!

IT'S HARD TO CHANGE DIRECTION IN MID-AIR.

BUDDY, I'M GOING TO CHANGE A LOT MORE THAN YOUR DIRECTION.

SNIP SNAP CRACK

SHICKA SHICKA WWHISSSHHH

SHOOF SHOOF SHOOF SHO

KRITCH KRUNCH KRITCH KRUNCH

SOMETIMES IT'S GOOD TO HUSH UP A WHILE AND LET AUTUMN STICK IN A FEW WORDS.

Hey, Calvin, c'mere.

SHOVE

Ha ha ha! What a weenie! Ha ha ha!

PEOPLE WHO GET NOSTALGIC ABOUT CHILDHOOD WERE OBVIOUSLY NEVER CHILDREN.

WATERSON

YOU LOOK DOWN IN THE DUMPS.

I AM.

MOE KEEPS KNOCKING ME DOWN AT SCHOOL FOR NO REASON. HE'S MEAN JUST FOR KICKS.

I SURE AM GLAD YOU'RE AN ANIMAL. ANIMALS SOMETIMES MAKE A LOT MORE SENSE THAN PEOPLE DO.

...AND WE'RE CUTER, TOO.

RIGHT, HOBBES. GOOD POINT.

WATERSON

LOOK, HOBBES, I NEED YOU TO COME TO SCHOOL WITH ME AND SHOW MOE A LITTLE FANG, OK?

YOU DON'T NEED TO KILL HIM OR ANYTHING. JUST GIVE 'IM SOMETHING TO THINK ABOUT ON THE WAY TO SURGERY.

HE USUALLY COMES AFTER ME AT RECESS, SO WE'LL GET HIM THEN. HEY, YOU DON'T HAVE RABIES, DO YOU?

CERTAINLY NOT.

RATS. WELL, I SUPPOSE HE'D AT LEAST HAVE TO GET A TETANUS SHOT.

WATERSON

HEY, CALVIN, WHY'D YOU BRING YOUR STUFFED TIGER TO SCHOOL? IT'S NOT A SHOW AND TELL DAY.

I KNOW. HOBBES IS GOING TO GIVE MOE A LITTLE "TREAT" TODAY: A RIDE IN AN AMBULANCE HELICOPTER.

YEAH? HOW'S HE GOING TO DO *THAT*?

IF YOU HAVE AN AVERSION TO DESCRIPTIONS OF CARNAGE, YOU PROBABLY DON'T WANT TO KNOW.

TALKING WITH YOU IS SORT OF THE CONVERSATIONAL EQUIVALENT OF AN OUT-OF-BODY EXPERIENCE.

DON'T GET TOO CLOSE NOW. I WANT HOBBES TO STAY FRESH FOR THIS AFTERNOON.

Look, Calvin's got a teddy bear. That's real sweet, Cal.

IT'S A TIGER, YOU BRAINLESS INVERTEBRATE.

Hey, maybe I'd like to play with your teddy!

GOOD IDEA, MOE. HOBBES PLAYS KINDA ROUGH, BUT HE'S *LOTS* OF FUN. C'MERE AND TAKE HIM.

Why? Is the teacher watching? This is a trick, right? I'm not touching your stupid teddy, see?

C'MON, I DARE YOU! WHAT'S THE MATTER? ARE YOU CHICKEN?

HA HA! BOY, YOU SURE SCARED *HIM* OFF! YOU WERE GREAT!

COME BACK AND CALL ME A "BEAR" AGAIN! YEAH, *YOU*, BUB!!

I CALLED YOUR TEACHER ABOUT MOE'S BULLYING, AND SHE SAID SHE'D PUT A STOP TO IT.

I'M AFRAID YOU WASTED YOUR TIME, MOM. MOE TOOK ONE LOOK AT HOBBES AND JUST ABOUT LOST HIS LUNCH!

I DON'T THINK MOE WILL BE BOTHERING *ME* FOR A WHILE. IT'S NOT EVERY KID WHO HAS A *TIGER* FOR A BEST FRIEND.

...AND WHAT LUCKY MOMS THOSE OTHER KIDS HAVE.

C'MON, HOBBES, IF YOU'LL LEND ME A BUCK, I'LL BUY YOU A COMIC BOOK.

PROCESSED LUNCH MEAT IS PRETTY SCARY. WHAT **ARE** THESE LITTLE SPECKS, ANYWAY? LIZARD PARTS? WHO KNOWS?

AND THIS "SKIN." I HEARD IT USED TO BE MADE OF INTESTINE, BUT I THINK NOWADAYS IT'S PLASTIC.

OF COURSE, THEY DYE AND WAX FRUIT SO IT LOOKS BETTER. IT'S LIKE EATING A CANDLE.

AND MOM WONDERS WHY I'M SO HUNGRY AFTER SCHOOL.

YEP, WE'D PROBABLY BE DEAD NOW IF IT WASN'T FOR TWINKIES.

HEY, DAD, YOUR LATEST POLL JUST CAME IN. LET'S SEE WHAT IT SAYS.

BE STILL, MY HEART.

WELL, I'LL BE! YOUR POPULARITY IS IMPROVING! YOU WENT UP 30 POINTS!

REALLY?

HECK, NO WONDER! I'M READING THE GRAPH UPSIDE-DOWN. WHAT A KLUTZ I AM!

...HOPE YOU'RE ALL PACKED, DAD.

DON'T YOU HAVE SOME HOMEWORK TO DO?

I LIKE TO MESS WITH HIS DREAMS.

ZZ...COOKIES? FOR ME? WHY SURE, BACK UP THE TRUCK... ZZZZ

85

STIR
STIR
STIR

STIR
STIR
STIR

I WON'T EAT ANY CEREAL THAT DOESN'T TURN THE MILK PURPLE.

THE DEADLY TORNADO MAKES ITS WAY ACROSS THE COMMUNITY!

THE CIRCLING UPDRAFT CLOCKS AT OVER 200 MPH! THE TWISTER SEARCHES FOR A TRAILER PARK!

FINDING ONE, IT TOUCHES DOWN! DEBRIS IS THROWN FOR MILES IN THE ENSUING EXPLOSION OF RUSHING AIR!

WHEN ARE YOU GOING TO CLEAN UP THIS ROOM?! IT LOOKS LIKE A...

TORNADO HIT IT, I KNOW.

OH BOY, IT'S SATURDAY!!

WHAT'S GOING ON? WHY AREN'T THERE ANY CARTOONS ON TV? IT'S JUST A TEST PATTERN.

THE TV GUIDE SAYS THEY DON'T START UNTIL 6:30.

HECK, THAT'S 45 MINUTES FROM NOW! WELL, C'MON, I'LL RACE YOU UP AND DOWN THE STAIRS!

WHY CAN'T HE EVER GET UP LIKE THIS ON SCHOOL DAYS?

GO BREAK HIS LITTLE LEGS, WILL YOU, HONEY?

BANG!
BONK

BAD NEWS ON YOUR CAMPAIGN TO STAY DAD, DAD.

OH?

YEP. THE LATEST POLL OF SIX-YEAR-OLDS IN THIS HOUSEHOLD SHOWS THAT THEY DON'T CARE ABOUT ISSUES THIS YEAR. IT'S CHARACTER THAT COUNTS.

SO WHY IS THAT BAD NEWS?

WHO'S THE BIMBO WITH YOU IN THIS OLD PROM PICTURE?

THAT "BIMBO" IS YOUR MOTHER!

WHO'S A BIMBO?!

PRETTY FUNKY HAIRDO, MOM!

IT'S THE SAD TRUTH, DAD. NOBODY CARES ABOUT YOUR POSITIONS ON FATHERHOOD. WE JUST WANT TO KNOW ABOUT YOUR CHARACTER.

IF YOU'RE GOING TO BE DAD HERE, WE HAVE TO KNOW YOU'VE NEVER DONE OR SAID ANYTHING THAT WOULD REFLECT POORLY ON YOUR JUDGMENT.

I HAVE YOUR COLLEGE YEARBOOK HERE. LET'S FLIP THROUGH IT, SHALL WE?

IS THIS YOU WITH THE KEG AND THE "PARTY NAKED" T-SHIRT?

GIVE ME THAAAT!

GRANDPA SAYS THE COMICS WERE A LOT BETTER YEARS AGO WHEN NEWSPAPERS PRINTED THEM BIGGER.

HE SAYS COMICS NOW ARE JUST A BUNCH OF XEROXED TALKING HEADS BECAUSE THERE'S NO SPACE TO TELL A DECENT STORY OR TO SHOW ANY ACTION.

HE THINKS PEOPLE SHOULD WRITE TO THEIR NEWSPAPERS AND COMPLAIN.

YOUR GRANDPA TAKES THE FUNNIES PRETTY SERIOUSLY.

YEAH, MOM'S LOOKING INTO NURSING HOMES.

DID YOU READ THIS? THIS TV STAR MADE OVER TWENTY MILLION DOLLARS LAST YEAR!

WHAT WOULD *YOU* DO WITH TWENTY MILLION BUCKS?

BEATS ME. I THINK IT'S RIDICULOUS THAT ANYONE MAKES THAT KIND OF MONEY.

OK, SAY YOU ONLY MADE *FIFTEEN* MILLION.

LET'S SAY EIGHTEEN.

HI, MOM.

BUM BA DA BUM BUM

WHAT'S COOKING?

HA HA HA HA HA HA!

WHAT'S WITH *YOU*?

I THOUGHT MY LIFE WOULD SEEM MORE INTERESTING WITH A MUSICAL SCORE AND A LAUGH TRACK.

I MADE UP A JOKE. A MAN'S GOING FOR A WALK, SO HE GETS HIS DOG AND SAYS, "HEEL!"

..AND THE DOG LOOKS UP AND SAYS, "IT TAKES ONE TO KNOW ONE, BUSTER!" HA HA HA HA HA!!

WHAT'S THE MATTER WITH YOU? DON'T YOU *GET* IT?!

AHHH, WHAT DO TIGERS KNOW ABOUT SOPHISTICATED HUMOR, ANYWAY?

HOW DID THE DOG LEARN TO TALK?

HI, SUSIE. WHAT DO YOU HAVE FOR LUNCH TODAY?

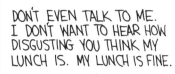
DON'T EVEN TALK TO ME. I DON'T WANT TO HEAR HOW DISGUSTING YOU THINK MY LUNCH IS. MY LUNCH IS FINE.

RELAX. I WASN'T GOING TO SAY A WORD ABOUT YOUR LUNCH. PASS ME SOME SALT, WILL YOU PLEASE?

HERE. THANKS. SLUGS ARE SO CHEWY BEFORE YOU SHRIVEL 'EM UP.

I'M HOME! BOINGGG

POW!

I READ THAT TIGERS' SPINAL COLUMNS ARE LIKE BIG COILED SPRINGS!

I READ THAT THEIR BRAINS ARE LIKE BIG BOWLS OF TAPIOCA.

BLECCHH! HOW LONG ARE THOSE TWO GONNA KEEP KISSING? THIS PROGRAM ONLY LASTS AN HOUR!

GEEZ, LOOK AT THEM SLOBBERING OVER EACH OTHER'S FACES! WHY WOULD ANYBODY *DO* THAT? DO THEY *LIKE* IT?

BED TIME.

THERE'S A CONNECTION HERE, I JUST KNOW IT.

QUIT HOGGING THE BED. YOU'RE WAY OVER ON MY SIDE.

TOUGH BEANS, FUZZ FACE.

EVER THINK ABOUT GEYSERS AND WATERFALLS? HUNDREDS OF THOUSANDS OF GALLONS OF WATER! FLOWING, SPILLING, RUSHING, GUSHING, SPLASHING!

HE REALLY FIGHTS MEAN.

SPACEMAN SPIFF FLEES THE DESPICABLE SCUM BEINGS OF PLANET Q-13!

IN A SURPRISE MANEUVER, OUR HERO TURNS TO FACE THE ADVERSARY! HIS HAND TIGHTENS AROUND THE DEATH RAY TRIGGER!

IT DOESN'T RESPOND! SPIFF REACHES FOR THE MERTILIZER BEAM, BUT IT DOESN'T WORK EITHER! NEITHER DO THE PHOSPHO BOMBS OR THE MORDO BLASTERS! NOTHING IS WORKING!!

1812! GETTYSBURG! 16 FLUID OUNCES! I BEFORE E! THOMAS EDISON!

PERHAPS SOME-ONE WHO HAS BEEN *PAYING ATTENTION* CAN HELP OUT CALVIN?

Z

YAAHH!

I KEEP FORGETTING THAT FIVE OF HIS SIX ENDS ARE POINTY WHEN HE LIES LIKE THAT.

SINCE SEPTEMBER, IT'S JUST GOTTEN COLDER AND COLDER.

THERE'S LESS DAYLIGHT NOW, I'VE NOTICED, TOO.

OH NO! THIS CAN ONLY MEAN ONE THING!

THE SUN IS GOING OUT! IN A FEW MORE MONTHS EARTH WILL BE A DARK AND LIFELESS BALL OF ICE!

WELL, GEE, NOW I DON'T FEEL SO BAD ABOUT NOT SETTING UP AN IRA LAST YEAR.

DAD SAYS THE SUN ISN'T GOING OUT.

HE SAYS IT'S COLDER BECAUSE OUR HEMISPHERE IS TILTED AWAY FROM THE SUN NOW.

HE SAYS WINTER WILL BE HERE SOON.

ISN'T IT SAD HOW SOME PEOPLE'S GRIP ON THEIR LIVES IS SO PRECARIOUS THAT THEY'LL EMBRACE ANY PREPOSTEROUS DELUSION RATHER THAN FACE AN OCCASIONAL BLEAK TRUTH?

ARE YOU GOING TO LIVE THE LAST FEW MONTHS OF YOUR LIFE ANY DIFFERENTLY, NOW THAT THE SUN IS GOING OUT AND WE'RE ALL DOOMED?

NO, I'VE ALWAYS BELIEVED IN LIVING EACH DAY AS IF IT WAS MY LAST, SO I NEVER HAVE ANY REGRETS.

KIND OF INSPIRING, HUH?

IF YOU WERE SOMEONE ELSE, IT MIGHT BE.

PASS ME THAT ISSUE OF CAPTAIN NAPALM, WILL YOU?

Calvin and Hobbes

by WATTERSON

BBWAAOHH

CALVIN, IT'S TIME TO WAKE UP.

Z

CALVIN, IT'S TIME TO WAKE UP.

C'MON, YOU'LL BE LATE FOR SCHOOL.

Z

MY DREAMS ARE GETTING WAY TOO LITERAL.

I ALWAYS WANTED TO BE A CUB SCOUT AND GET MERIT BADGES AND STUFF, BUT I HATE GOING TO MEETINGS.

OK OK, JUST READ ABOUT KNOTS, ALL RIGHT?

HEY, LOOK, HERE'S A MOTTO! I DIDN'T KNOW YOU HAD A MOTTO! WOW, WHAT FUN!

"LIVE FOR REVENGE" IS GOING TO BE MY MOTTO IF YOU DON'T GET ME OUT OF THIS.

WATTERSON

I'LL QUIZ YOU. WHAT DO YOU DO FOR A SECOND-DEGREE BURN?

DON'T FLIP THROUGH THE BOOK, YOU IDIOT! UNTIE ME!

HMPH, IF I WAS IN YOUR PREDICAMENT, I'D TREAT ME WITH A LOT MORE RESPECT. DO YOU SAY YOU'RE SORRY?

MMFF! RRGGH! OOH! ARGH! YOU DIRTY ROTTEN STINKING

HOBBES, I'M NOT KIDDING. IF YOU DON'T GET ME LOOSE IN TEN SECONDS...

YOU GOT YOURSELF INTO THIS, "MR. HOUDINI," NOT ME.

BUT I'M SUPPOSED TO BE AT DINNER! MOM'S GONNA KILL ME!

ESCAPE ARTISTS HAVE A RISKY TRADE. HEY, HERE'S MORSE CODE!

OK, I'M SORRY I CALLED YOU NAMES. I SAID I'M SORRY, RIGHT? NOW UNTIE ME!

HERE'S HOW YOU SAY "BANANA" IN MORSE. DASH DOT DOT DOT, DOT DASH...

WATTERSON

WHAT IS THAT KID DOING?! IT SOUNDS LIKE A CHAIR THUMPING AROUND THE ROOM.

WELL, HIS DINNER IS STONE COLD. I HOPE HE'S HAPPY.

BONK BONK

ALL RIGHT, YOUNG MAN! YOU'VE WASTED THE NICE MEAL YOUR MOM FIXED. GET OUT HERE.

WATTERSON

YOU TIED YOURSELF UP?? WHAT ON EARTH WERE YOU DOING?!

HOBBES TIED ME UP, DAD! IT'S HIS FAULT!

DON'T MAKE UP LIES, CALVIN. HOW DID YOU GET YOURSELF LIKE THIS?!

HOBBES DID IT, DAD! HE WAS GOING TO HOLD ME FOR RANSOM! HONEST!

RANSOM?? WHO'D PAY FOR YOU, YOU BIG FIBBER?! I'M CERTAINLY GLAD YOUR DAD SAW THROUGH THAT FILTHY LIE!

OH, HUSH. YOU ALWAYS GET ME IN TROUBLE.

98

CALVIN and HOBBES by WATTERSON

First there was nothing...

...then there was Calvin!

Calvin, the mighty god, creates the universe with pure will!

From utter nothingness comes swirling form! Life begins where once was void!

But Calvin is no kind and loving god! He's one of the old gods! He demands sacrifice!

Yes, Calvin is a god of the underworld! And the puny inhabitants of earth displease him!

The great Calvin ignores their pleas for mercy and the doomed writhe in agony!

HAVE YOU SEEN HOW ABSORBED CALVIN IS WITH THOSE TINKERTOYS? HE'S CREATING WHOLE WORLDS OVER THERE!

I'LL BET HE GROWS UP TO BE AN ARCHITECT.

What's for dinner, Mom?

Tortellini.

Oh, no, not tortellini! I HATE tortellini!! Oh, gross! Yecch! Tortellini!!

Nothing is more disgusting than tortellini!! Can't we have something else?

No.

Tortellini... tortellini... T-O-R...

Did you see we have a substitute teacher today?

Oh, no! That can only mean our REAL teacher rocketed back to Saturn to report to her superiors!

They're trying to subvert us little kids with subliminal messages in our textbooks, telling us to turn in our parents when the Saturnians attack! Earth will be rendered helpless!

I think one of us has been eating too much paste in art class.

I'm too smart for 'em, though! I don't read my assignments!

Behold the terrible thunder lizard, Tyrannosaurus Rex!

The fiercest dinosaur of all, he is twenty tons of bone-crushing muscle and razor-sharp teeth!

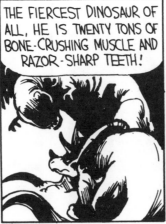

Always the victor, he lets out a triumphant roar!

BOOT

LIBRARY

AH.. **AH..** AH.. ∞

I JUTH **HADE** IT WHED THITH HAPPEDTH.

CALVIN THE CRIMINAL IS ABOUT TO FACE JUSTICE! ANGRY THRONGS TURN OUT TO WATCH HIS EXECUTION!

AS HE IS LED UP THE GALLOWS, HE REFLECTS UPON HIS MANY HEINOUS CRIMES. HE IS NOT REPENTANT!

THE NOOSE IS PUT AROUND HIS NECK AND TIGHTENED! THIS IS THE END!

GACKK URRGHH

OH, KNOCK IT OFF. SOME OF US HAVE TO WEAR A TIE EVERY DAY.

HOW WAS THE KIDDY MATINEE MOVIE?

MOVIE? OH, YEAH, THE MOVIE. YEAH, THERE WAS A MOVIE. IT WAS OK, I GUESS.

HOW WAS THE MATINEE?

WE... ARE... BUYING... A VIDEO PLAYER.

CalViN aNd HObbES
by WATTERSON

YAWN

PUTT PUTT PUTT PUTT PUTT PUTT

Z

SCRITCH SCRATCH

ZZ
MMM..

RUB RUB RUB

ZZ
..RRRR..

SHOOF SHOOF SHOOF

ZZ
.OOO..MM..

ITCH ITCH ITCH ITCH

ZZ
YOW WOW
YOW WOW
ZZ..

NKG
K
ZZ..

HMMMMM

ZZZ
Z

THAT SIGH OUGHT TO GET ME OUT OF A FEW YEARS' PURGATORY.

Z

Dear Santa.

Attached is my Christmas list for this year.

Last year I did not receive several items from my List.

For your convenience, I have grouped those items together on page 12. Please check them carefully, and include them with the rest of my loot this year.

THAT'S THE PROBLEM WITH THIS GUY. HE'S GOTTEN SLOPPY WITHOUT ANY COMPETITION.

HE SEES YOU WHEN YOU'RE SLEEPING, HE KNOWS WHEN YOU'RE AWAKE ...

HE KNOWS IF YOU'VE BEEN BAD OR GOOD, SO BE GOOD FOR GOODNESS SAKE!

* CLICK *

SANTA CLAUS: KINDLY OLD ELF, OR CIA SPOOK?

THIS SANTA CLAUS STUFF BOTHERS ME.... ESPECIALLY THE JUDGE AND JURY BIT.

WHO APPOINTED SANTA? HOW DO WE KNOW HE'S IMPARTIAL? WHAT CRITERIA DOES HE USE FOR DETERMINING GOOD AND BAD?

AND WHAT ABOUT EXTENUATING CIRCUMSTANCES? KIDS SHOULD HAVE THE BENEFIT OF LEGAL COUNSEL, DON'T YOU THINK?

YOU'RE WORRIED ABOUT THE SALAMANDER INCIDENT, AREN'T YOU?

TEMPORARY INSANITY! THAT'S ALL IT WAS!

THEY SAY SANTA KNOWS IF YOU'VE BEEN GOOD OR BAD, BUT WHAT IF SOMEONE HAD BEEN SORT OF *BOTH*?

I MEAN, SUPPOSE SOME KID *TRIED* TO BE GOOD...AT LEAST, WELL, MOST OF THE TIME...BUT BAD THINGS INEXPLICABLY KEPT HAPPENING?

SUPPOSE SOME KID JUST HAD TERRIBLE LUCK, AND HE GOT BLAMED FOR A LOT OF THINGS HE DID ONLY *SORT* OF ON PURPOSE?

WHO EXACTLY MIGHT WE BE TALKING ABOUT?

THIS IS A PURELY HYPOTHETICAL CASE, MR. SMARTY PANTS.

THIS WHOLE SANTA CLAUS THING JUST DOESN'T MAKE SENSE.

WHY ALL THE SECRECY? WHY ALL THE MYSTERY? IF THE GUY EXISTS, WHY DOESN'T HE EVER SHOW HIMSELF AND PROVE IT?

AND IF HE *DOESN'T* EXIST, WHAT'S THE MEANING OF ALL THIS?

I DUNNO... ISN'T THIS A RELIGIOUS HOLIDAY?

YEAH, BUT ACTUALLY, I'VE GOT THE SAME QUESTIONS ABOUT GOD.

GOSH, HOBBES, WHAT IF I DON'T GET ANY PRESENTS THIS YEAR BECAUSE I DOUBTED THE EXISTENCE OF SANTA?

SUPPOSE HE'S PUTTING MY NAME ON THE "BAD" LIST RIGHT NOW! THAT WOULD BE AWFUL!

PERSONALLY, I'D THINK THAT IF YOU WEREN'T ON THE "BAD" LIST ALL ALONG, THIS WOULDN'T PUSH YOU OVER.

THANKS FOR THE COMFORT, EGGNOG BRAIN.

SEE? *SEE* WHY YOU'RE ON THE "BAD" LIST? INSULTS!

HERE'S A BOX OF CRAYONS. I NEED SOME ILLUSTRATIONS FOR A STORY I'M WRITING.

YOU CAN DRAW SOMETHING BESIDES TIGERS, CAN'T YOU?

SURE. LEOPARDS, PUMAS, OCELOTS.. ..YOU NAME IT.

HERE, DAD, READ *THIS* STORY TONIGHT. I WROTE IT AND HOBBES ILLUSTRATED IT.

..UM... OK.

"THE DAD WHO LIVED TO REGRET BEING MEAN TO HIS KID."

WHAT ARE YOU PAUSING FOR? KEEP READING.

Barney's dad was really bad, So Barney hatched a plan. When his dad said, "Eat your peas!" Barney shouted, "NO!" and ran.

peas

Barney

Barney tricked his mean ol' dad, And locked him in the cellar. His mom never found out where he'd gone, 'Cause Barney didn't tell her.

door

key

There his dad spent his life, Eating mice and gruel. With every bite for fifty years He was sorry he'd been cruel. THE END.

Barney's dad

mice

YOU KNOW HOW A LOT OF STORIES HAVE MORALS TO THEM...?

I *GET* IT, I *GET* IT!

WATTERSON & HOBS

WHAT DO YOU THINK IS THE MEANING OF TRUE HAPPINESS?

IS IT MONEY, CARS AND WOMEN?

..OR IS IT JUST MONEY AND CARS?

WELL-L-L-L?

LOOK AT THIS! YOU CALL THIS SNOW?!

IT'S NOT EVEN AN INCH HIGH! WHAT GOOD IS LESS THAN AN INCH OF SNOW?!

WELL, IT'S PRETTY.

NOBODY EVER CLOSED A SCHOOL ON ACCOUNT OF PRETTINESS.

THIS WILL BE THE STRONGEST SNOW FORT EVER MADE!

KEEP PACKING ON SNOW. THIS WILL BE INDESTRUCTIBLE.

WE'LL POUR WATER ON IT, SO IT FREEZES OVERNIGHT. THAT WAY OUR FORT WILL BE HERE UNTIL JULY!

WHERE'S THAT KID?!

THIS SNOW FORT CAN REPEL ANY ATTACK!

I HATE THIS NEIGHBORHOOD.

WHAP!

I'M GLAD TO SEE *YOU'RE* INSIDE.

IT'S HANDY NOT TO HAVE BOOTS AND A COAT TO TAKE OFF.

MY SNOW FORT MAKES ME INVULNERABLE!

FROM BEHIND ITS THICK WALL, I CAN LAUNCH A BRUTAL SNOWBALL BARRAGE AND REMAIN SAFE FROM RETALIATION!

WHAP!

YOU'RE SUPPOSED TO ATTACK FROM *THAT* SIDE OF THE FORT, DUMMY!!

I HATE WAITING FOR THE SCHOOL BUS ON DAYS LIKE THESE.

BLUSTERY COLD DAYS SHOULD BE SPENT PROPPED UP IN BED WITH A MUG OF HOT CHOCOLATE AND A PILE OF COMIC BOOKS.

THAT'S WHAT I'D LIKE TO BE DOING RIGHT NOW.

AS SOON AS I GRADUATE, I'M GOING TO SPEND *EVERY* WINTER THAT WAY.

I WISH YOUR BUS WOULD COME. MY HOT CHOCOLATE WILL GET COLD.

HELP ME FIGURE OUT THIS HOME-WORK PROBLEM, HOBBES. WHAT'S 3 + 8 ?

OK, ASSIGN THE ANSWER A VALUE OF "X". "X" ALWAYS MEANS MULTIPLY, SO TAKE THE NUMERATOR (THAT'S LATIN FOR "NUMBER EIGHTER") AND PUT THAT ON THE OTHER SIDE OF THE EQUATION.

THAT LEAVES YOU WITH THREE ON THIS SIDE, SO WHAT TIMES THREE EQUALS EIGHT? THE ANSWER, OF COURSE, IS SIX.

GOSH, I MUST HAVE DONE ALL THE OTHERS WRONG.

THESE PROBLEMS SEEM AWFULLY ADVANCED FOR FIRST GRADE, IF YOU ASK ME.

HERE'S ANOTHER MATH PROBLEM I CAN'T FIGURE OUT. WHAT'S 9 + 4 ?

OOH, THAT'S A TRICKY ONE. YOU HAVE TO USE CALCULUS AND IMAGINARY NUMBERS FOR THIS.

IMAGINARY NUMBERS?!

YOU KNOW, ELEVENTEEN, THIRTY-TWELVE, AND ALL THOSE. IT'S A LITTLE CONFUSING AT FIRST.

HOW DID *YOU* LEARN ALL THIS? YOU'VE NEVER EVEN GONE TO SCHOOL!

INSTINCT. TIGERS ARE BORN WITH IT.

IT'S FREEZING IN THIS HOUSE! SOMEBODY CRANK UP THE THERMOSTAT! WHY DOESN'T SOMEONE MAKE A FIRE?!

IF WE CAN'T AFFORD TO HEAT THIS PLACE, MAYBE DAD SHOULD GET A BETTER JOB! WHY CAN'T WE MOVE TO FLORIDA?!

CALVIN, PIPE DOWN AND PUT ON A SWEATER IF YOU'RE COLD.

AND GO TO ALL THAT TROUBLE?!

WATERSON

I READ THAT THE AVERAGE HOUSEHOLD WATCHES 7½ HOURS OF TV EVERY DAY.

MOM SAYS SHE DOESN'T WATCH TV AT ALL WHILE I'M AT SCHOOL...

...SO IF I GET HOME AT 3:00, I SHOULD BE ABLE TO WATCH IT STRAIGHT TILL 10:30, RIGHT?

WRONG.

DO YOU WANT US TO BE SUB-AVERAGE?!

WATERSON

MOM, THE WASHER IS DONE.

OK.

AREN'T YOU GOING TO PUT THE WASH IN THE DRYER?

IN A MINUTE.

YOU MEAN YOU'RE JUST GOING TO LET IT SIT IN THE WASHING MACHINE?!?

CALVIN, CAN'T YOU SEE I'M BUSY RIGHT NOW??

SHE SAYS SHE'S BUSY.

I HOPE THE NEXT TIME SHE TAKES A BATH THERE AREN'T ANY TOWELS.

WATERSON

WHO'S COMING TO VISIT?

YOUR UNCLE MAX. I THOUGHT I TOLD YOU.

UNCLE MAX ?? **I** DON'T REMEMBER ANY UNCLE MAX. ARE YOU SURE HE'S RELATED? MAYBE HE'S A CON MAN TRYING TO SWINDLE US!

OF COURSE HE'S RELATED. HE'S YOUR DAD'S BROTHER. HE JUST HASN'T BEEN HERE FOR A FEW YEARS.

WHY NOT? WAS HE IN JAIL?

NO! GOOD HEAVENS, CALVIN.

NOW, NOW... WITH MAX, THAT'S NOT A BAD GUESS.

WE'RE GETTING NEAR THE AIRPORT, CALVIN. SEE THE JETS?

HOW COME YOU'RE SO QUIET BACK THERE? AREN'T YOU EXCITED TO SEE UNCLE MAX?

...YEAH...

I JUST HOPE NOBODY THINKS I'M GIVING UP **MY** ROOM WHILE HE'S HERE.

IT'S GREAT TO SEE YOU, MAX! IT SEEMS LIKE AGES SINCE YOU'VE BEEN HERE.

I'LL SAY.

I DIDN'T THINK IT HAD BEEN SO LONG, UNTIL I SAW CALVIN. THIS GUY HAS REALLY GROWN.

SO KID, WHAT DO YOU SAY?

I SAY YOU'D BETTER WATCH YOUR STEP, 'CAUSE I'VE GOT A LIVE, MAN-EATING TIGER AT HOME, AND IF I SO MUCH AS WINK, HE'LL RIP YOUR LUNGS OUT.

CUTE KID, BRO.

Calvin and Hobbes

by WATTERSON

I'VE GOT TO GO IN. ANOTHER FIVE MINUTES OUT HERE, AND I'LL BE FROZEN SOLID.

GOSH, I HOPE THAT WAS NO ONE I KNEW.

YOU LOOKED PRETTY COLD COMING UP THE HILL, SO I FIXED YOU SOME HOT CHOCOLATE AND CRACKERS WITH PEANUT BUTTER.

GO WRAP UP IN A BLANKET AND TAKE THESE IN FRONT OF THE FIRE.

HERE'S HOBBES AND A COMIC BOOK. GETTING TOASTY?

UH HUH. THANKS.

SHE EVEN PUT MARSHMALLOWS IN THE HOT CHOCOLATE.

NOBODY KNOWS HOW TO PAMPER LIKE A MOM.

SO ARE YOU GOING TO EAT ALL THOSE PEANUT BUTTER CRACKERS YOURSELF, OR WHAT?

WATTERSON

WE HAVE TO GIVE OUR REPORT ON PLANET MERCURY TODAY. DID YOU DO YOUR HALF?

OF COURSE I DID. AND I'LL BET MY HALF MAKES YOUR HALF LOOK PATHETIC.

IT HAD **BETTER** BE GOOD... OR ELSE!

THE PLANET MERCURY
An Exhaustively Researched Report by Calvin

".. AND SO, THE PLANET MERCURY IS A HOT AND BARREN WORLD, THE CLOSEST TO OUR SUN."

AND TO TELL US ABOUT THE MYTHOLOGY OF MERCURY, HERE'S MY PARTNER, CALVIN.

THANK YOU, THANK YOU! HEY, WHAT A CROWD! YOU LOOK GREAT THIS MORNING... REALLY, I MEAN THAT! GO ON, GIVE YOURSELVES A HAND!

YOU KNOW, A FUNNY THING HAPPENED ON THE WAY TO THE LIBRARY YESTERDAY...

THIS ISN'T MY FAULT, MISS WORMWOOD!

THE PLANET MERCURY WAS NAMED AFTER A ROMAN GOD WITH WINGED FEET.

MERCURY WAS THE GOD OF FLOWERS AND BOUQUETS, WHICH IS WHY TODAY HE IS A REGISTERED TRADEMARK OF FTD FLORISTS.

WHY THEY NAMED A PLANET AFTER THIS GUY, I CAN'T IMAGINE.

... UM... BACK TO YOU, SUSIE.

BOY, YOU SHOULD'VE SEEN THE SPARKS FLY WHEN I GAVE MY HALF OF THE REPORT.

I'VE NEVER SEEN SUSIE SO MAD. SHE ACCUSED ME OF NOT DOING ANY RESEARCH AND CLAIMED I MADE UP THE WHOLE THING.

DID YOU?

HECK, NO. I JUST TOOK A FEW CREATIVE LIBERTIES.

AND THEY CALLED YOUR MOM OVER A FEW CREATIVE LIBERTIES?

GEEZ, YOU THINK *SUSIE* WAS MAD...

DON'T YOU HATE IT WHEN YOUR BOOGERS FREEZE?

HERE WE ARE, OVERLOOKING SUICIDE GULCH, ABOUT TO HURL OURSELVES DOWN AT BREAKNECK SPEED IN A SLED THAT HARDLY STEERS!

RISKING LIFE AND LIMB! LOOKING DEATH STRAIGHT IN THE EYE!

"WHY?" YOU ASK! WHY DO WE DO IT??

BECAUSE WE GET PAID, I HOPE.

BECAUSE IT'S THERE!

LOOK, HOBBES, THE LATEST PERFECTION IN TECHNOLOGY.

A WATER PISTOL?

HECK, NO! THIS IS THE NEW, IMPROVED VERSION OF THE TRANSMOGRIFIER.

NOW YOU CAN TRANSMOGRIFY THINGS JUST BY POINTING AT THEM! SAY YOU DON'T LIKE THE COLOR OF YOUR BEDSPREAD. WELL, YOU JUST ZAP IT, AND PRESTO, IT'S AN IGUANA!

ONE CAN CERTAINLY IMAGINE THE MYRIAD OF USES FOR A HAND-HELD IGUANA MAKER.

IT DOESN'T *HAVE* TO BE AN IGUANA. IT CAN BE ANYTHING. SUPPOSE MOM'S GETTING ON OUR NERVES, FOR INSTANCE...

HOW DOES THIS TRANSMOGRIFIER GUN KNOW WHAT TO TRANSMOGRIFY SOMETHING INTO?

TELEPATHY.

THE GUN AUTOMATICALLY READS THE BRAIN WAVES YOU EMIT, AND TURNS THE OBJECT INTO WHATEVER YOU WANT.

THAT'S AMAZING.

WELL, IT TOOK ME ALL MORNING TO INVENT.

SO SAY I'M THINKING ABOUT A BIG SLAB OF GRILLED TUNA NOW...

WATCH WHERE YOU'RE POINTING THAT! WATCH WHERE YOU'RE POINTING THAT!

OK, LET'S TEST THIS TRANSMOGRIFIER GUN.

I WANT TO BE A PTERODACTYL, SO YOU THINK OF ONE AND POINT THE TRANSMOGRIFIER AT ME.

THIS WILL BE GREAT. I'LL TERRORIZE THE NEIGHBORHOOD AWHILE AND THEN YOU CAN TRANSMOGRIFY ME BACK TO A BOY WHEN THE NATIONAL GUARD COMES.

WHAT'S A PTERODACTYL? SOME KIND OF BUG?

NO NO! IT'S A BIG FLYING DINOSAUR! DON'T SHOOT IF YOU DON'T KNOW WHAT IT IS!!

128

CaLViN and HobbES

by WATTERSON

WHAT AM I GOING TO DO, HOBBES? I CAN'T BE AN OWL FOREVER!

HOW AM I GOING TO TRANSMOGRIFY BACK INTO A KID WHEN THE TRANSMOGRIFIER IS BROKEN?

MAYBE YOU SHOULD JUST LEARN TO ACCEPT THIS PREDICAMENT. IT'S NOT SO BAD BEING AN OWL INSTEAD OF A KID. ACTUALLY, IT'S PROBABLY BETTER.

BETTER? HOW?

WELL, I NEVER QUITE KNEW HOW TO SAY THIS BEFORE, BUT LITTLE BOYS DON'T SMELL SO GOOD.

I'VE GOT TO GO TO SCHOOL TOMORROW MORNING! WHAT WILL THE KIDS SAY IF I'M AN OWL?!

OH, NO, I'M DOOMED! I'M DOOMED!

SINCE WHEN DO OWLS GO TO SCHOOL?

ZIP-A-DEE-DOO-DAH ZIP-A-DEE-AY! MY OH MY, WHAT A WONDERFUL DAY!

TIME TO GET UP, CALVIN. YOU DON'T WANT TO MISS THE SCHOOL BUS.

I'M NOT GOING TO SCHOOL, MOM. I'M AN OWL.

NO, YOU'RE NOT. NOW GET UP AND GET DRESSED.

I'M NOT AN OWL?

I'M NOT! I'M ME AGAIN! THE TRANSMOGRIFICATION MUST ONLY BE TEMPORARY! IT WORE OFF OVERNIGHT! I'M A KID! I CAN...

...GO...TO... SCHOOL.

..YAWWWNN.. KEEP THE SHADE DOWN WHEN YOU GO, OK?

DING DONG

I'LL GET IT.

HOBBES, QUICK! CLOSE THE CURTAINS AND HELP ME PROP FURNITURE AGAINST THE DOOR!

...IT'S ROSALYN!

DAD! DAD! WHERE DO YOU KEEP YOUR GUNS? GET OUT THE MAGNUM!

I DON'T HAVE ANY GUNS. WHAT'S THE PROBLEM?

ROSALYN'S HERE AND SHE WON'T GO AWAY! WHY ON EARTH DON'T YOU HAVE ANY GUNS??

YOUR MOM AND I ARE GOING OUT. ROSALYN IS HERE TO BABY-SIT.

DON'T YOU REMEMBER? I TOLD YOU THAT THIS MORNING.

YOU JUST DON'T PAY ATTENTION. THAT'S WHY YOU NEVER KNOW WHAT'S GOING ON.

HOW ABOUT A WOODEN STAKE AND A MALLET? DO WE HAVE THAT?!

CAN YOU BELIEVE IT, HOBBES? MOM AND DAD ASKED ROSALYN TO BABY-SIT US!

THERE'S JUST ONE THING TO DO. WE'LL MAIL OUR-SELVES TO AUSTRALIA. CLIMB IN.

JUST PUT US OUT BY THE MAIL-BOX, MOM.

STOP BEING SILLY, CALVIN. WHERE'S ROSALYN? I THOUGHT YOU SAID SHE WAS HERE.

AS FAR AS I KNOW, SHE'S STILL ON THE FRONT PORCH. WHY?

YOU DIDN'T EVEN LET HER IN?!

DING DONG DING DONG

134

135

Hey, Calvin, guess what we're doing in gym today. We're wrestling!

Next period you'll be so covered with mat burns you'll need skin grafts! Ha ha ha! See ya then, twinky.

SiGHHHHH...

PHYSICAL EDUCATION IS WHAT YOU LEARN FROM HAVING YOUR FACE IN SOMEONE'S ARMPIT RIGHT BEFORE LUNCH.

KAPWIINGGG!
IT'S CALVIN, THE HUMAN LIGHT PARTICLE!

IN THE BLINK OF AN EYE, HE'S 165,000 MILES AWAY!

NOTHING IN THE UNIVERSE IS FASTER THAN CALVIN!

...I HOPE!

MUCH AS I LOVE MY "CHOCOLATE FROSTED CRUNCHY SUGAR BOMBS," THE BEST PART IS AFTER THE CEREAL IS GONE.

THAT'S WHEN YOU EAT THE LEFTOVER MILK THAT'S ALL SLUDGY FROM THE EXTRA SUGAR YOU ADDED.

SOMETIMES I EAT TWO OR THREE BOWLS OF THIS.

I CAN HEAR YOUR HEART RACING FROM HERE.

THEY MAKE THIS CEREAL WITH MARSHMALLOW BITS, TOO, BUT MOM WON'T BUY IT FOR ME.

HEY, CALVIN! GUESS WHAT TIME IT IS!

WHY? WHAT TIME IS IT?

IT'S A VERY *SPECIAL* TIME!

OH BOY, OH BOY! WHAT TIME IS IT?

DO YOU *REALLY* WANT TO KNOW?

YES, YES! TELL ME! TELL ME! QUICK! PLEASE! YES!

IT'S YOUR BATH TIME! OH BOY!!

YOU KNOW HOW OLD PEOPLE ALWAYS WRITE TO DEAR ABBY, COMPLAINING THAT THEIR KIDS NEVER WRITE, CALL OR VISIT? THOSE LETTERS REALLY CRACK ME UP.

I HATE BEING A KID.

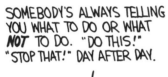

SOMEBODY'S ALWAYS TELLING YOU WHAT TO DO OR WHAT *NOT* TO DO. "DO THIS!" "STOP THAT!" DAY AFTER DAY.

YOU'RE LUCKY YOU'RE A TIGER.

WELL, WE TRY TO STAY HUMBLE, BUT LORD KNOWS IT'S HARD.

I WONDER IF I CAN GROW FANGS WHEN MY BABY TEETH FALL OUT.

I WISH *I* WAS A TIGER.

A COMMON LAMENT.

I'VE GOT AN IDEA! YOU CAN *TEACH* ME TO BE A TIGER! I'VE GOT SOME RED SLEEPERS I CAN WEAR! HANG ON!

SEE? WE CAN MAKE A TAIL BY STUFFING A KNEE SOCK AND PINNING IT ON MY REAR! THEN YOU CAN DRAW STRIPES ON MY FACE!

HMM... WHAT ABOUT FUR AND WHISKERS?

I HAVEN'T SHAVED FOR SIX YEARS. I SEEM TO BE CURSED WITH A THIN BEARD.

MY SIDE OF THE WOODS ABOUNDS IN NATURAL SCENIC SPLENDOR.

YOUR SIDE WALLOWS IN DECAY AND FILTH. MY TERRITORY IS INFINITELY SUPERIOR TO YOURS.

YOUR SIDE IS SMALLER.

HEY!

I'M HUNGRY.

WELL, YOU CAN'T CATCH ANYTHING IN MY TERRITORY. THAT'S WHAT THE BOOK SAYS.

WHAT DO TIGERS EAT IN THE WILD ANYWAY?

THEY CATCH BIG GROSS CATERPILLARS LIKE THAT ONE.

EWWW. IT'S GOT LITTLE SPIKES ALL OVER HIM. TIGERS REALLY EAT THESE?

BY THE TRUCK LOAD. THEY'RE GREAT.

LET ME SEE THE BOOK.

WHO ARE YOU GOING TO BELIEVE, SOME SILLY WRITER OR A REAL TIGER?

SO FAR, I HAVEN'T HAD MUCH FUN AS A TIGER.

I THOUGHT WE'D BE ROMPING AROUND THE WOODS LIKE WE ALWAYS DO, BUT IT TURNS OUT TIGERS DON'T SHARE THEIR TERRITORIES WITH OTHER TIGERS!

SO HERE WE ARE, SITTING ON OPPOSITE SIDES OF A BIG ROCK. WHAT A BLAST.

BEING A TIGER JUST ISN'T ALL IT'S CRACKED UP TO BE.

THAT'S NOT THE HALF OF IT. IT SAYS HERE WE'RE AN ENDANGERED SPECIES!

CALVIN and HOBBES by WATTERSON

THE LATE CRETACEOUS PERIOD...
WHEN DINOSAURS RULED THE EARTH!

..AND CALVIN RULED THE DINOSAURS!

THE TERRIBLE TYRANNOSAURUS SINKS ITS TEETH INTO A TRICERATOPS!

TRIUMPHANT AGAIN, THE UNDISPUTED KING OF DINOSAURS LETS OUT A MIGHTY ROAR!

WITH SAVAGE FEROCITY, THE MONSTER BEGINS ITS FEAST! LIMB-SEVERING, BONE-CRUNCHING AND TENDON-SNAPPING, HE...

CALVIN! THAT'S DISGUSTING!

FOR HEAVEN'S SAKE, SLOW DOWN AND CHEW QUIETLY!

THE TERRIBLE TYRANNOSAURUS RESUMES EATING, MORTIFIED THAT SOMEONE MIGHT SEE HIM.

UH OH, I'LL BET HOBBES IS WAITING TO SPRING ON ME AS SOON AS I OPEN THE FRONT DOOR!

I KNOW! I'LL SNEAK AROUND BACK AND SURPRISE *HIM!*

HEH HEH! THERE HE IS, ALL READY TO POUNCE! WHAT A SUCKER!

I'M HOME!

I'VE GOT TO START LISTENING TO THOSE QUIET, NAGGING DOUBTS.

LIGHTNING FLASHES!
THUNDER RUMBLES ACROSS
THE SKY!

HORRIBLY, CALVIN HAS BEEN
SEWN TOGETHER FROM
CORPSES! A POWER SURGE
FORCES BLOOD TO HIS BRAIN!

HE'S... HE'S
ALIVE!

WELL, LOOK
WHO'S UP AND
ABOUT.

HELLO,
SLEEPYHEAD.

..OGGG...

CALVIN WAKES UP STARING
INTO THE EYES OF A BIG
FROG.

SEEING CALVIN AWAKE, THE
FROG SCRAMBLES DOWN AND
FORCES OPEN CALVIN'S
MOUTH!

CALVIN TRIES TO FIGHT, BUT
THE SLIPPERY AMPHIBIAN
INSTANTLY SLIDES IN AND IS
SWALLOWED! HOW DISGUSTING!

I DON'T
FEEL
GOOD.

YOU SOUND
AWFUL. YOU'VE
GOT A FROG IN
YOUR THROAT.

CALVIN THE ELEPHANT
WANDERS THE AFRICAN
PLAIN.

AT FIVE TONS, HE IS THE
LARGEST LAND MAMMAL!

HIS DEAFENING CALL
SHATTERS THE EARLY-
MORNING TRANQUILITY!

151

HERE I AM, WAITING FOR THE BUS. ELEVEN MORE YEARS OF SCHOOL TO GO. THEN COLLEGE, THEN MAYBE GRADUATE SCHOOL, AND THEN I WORK UNTIL I DIE.

WHAT KIND OF WORLD *IS* THIS?! YOU ONLY GET FIVE YEARS TO BE A KID??

WHAT ABOUT EXPLORING AND DISCOVERING AND PLAYING? THOSE THINGS ARE IMPORTANT, TOO!

WELL, YOU STILL HAVE AFTERNOONS AND WEEKENDS.

THAT'S WHEN I WATCH TV.

LOOK, HOBBES, I GOT A MODEL AIRPLANE. WANT TO HELP ME BUILD IT?

SURE.

WOW, A PHANTOM JET! I CAN'T WAIT UNTIL IT'S DONE!

LOOK AT ALL THE LITTLE PIECES.

HERE, YOU PUT THOSE PIECES TOGETHER, AND I'LL DO THESE. THEN WE'LL STICK YOURS ON MINE, OK?

SHOULDN'T WE READ THE INSTRUCTIONS?

DO I *LOOK* LIKE A SISSY?

HEY, THESE INSTRUCTIONS ARE IN THREE DIFFERENT LANGUAGES.

UH OH, I GOT GLUE ON MY HANDS.

IT STARTS IN ENGLISH, BUT THEN IT GOES INTO FRENCH AND SPANISH.

THIS STUFF IS WORSE THAN MOZZARELLA CHEESE.

IT'S HARD TO BELIEVE THIS MODEL IS FOR AGES SIX AND UP.

YECCHH. WHAT A MESS.

YOU HAVE TO BE TRI-LINGUAL JUST TO READ THE DIRECTIONS.

I HOPE MOM LIKES THIS NEWSPAPER HERE ON THE FLOOR, BECAUSE IT'S SURE NOT GOING ANYWHERE.

NUTS! THIS WHEEL STRUT SNAPPED. WHY DO THEY MAKE 'EM SO DARN SMALL?

I GUESS THAT WAS AN OPTIONAL PIECE.

MY WHEEL WON'T FIT IN THE WHEEL WELL.

HERE, LET ME TRY. SOMETIMES YOU JUST HAVE TO...

SNAP

DARN IT!

THIS PLANE IS IN FOR SOME ROUGH LANDINGS.

LOOK AT THIS STUPID MODEL. IT LOOKS AWFUL!

OUR PLANE DOESN'T LOOK ANYTHING LIKE THE PICTURE ON THE BOX.

MAYBE WE CAN FIX IT WHEN WE PAINT IT.

I CAN'T PAINT IT LIKE THIS. LOOK HOW GOOD THEY DID THIS!

HOW'D THEY PAINT EYEBROWS ON A PILOT THAT'S LESS THAN AN INCH TALL ??

I THINK THAT'S A REAL JET SUPERIMPOSED ON A PLASTIC STAND.

I HATE THIS MODEL. NOTHING FIT RIGHT, THE INSTRUCTIONS WERE INCOMPREHENSIBLE, THE DECALS RIPPED, THE PAINT SLOPPED, AND THE GLUE GOT EVERYWHERE.

WHAT A DISASTER. SIX BUCKS COMPLETELY DOWN THE DRAIN.

I CAN'T THINK OF AN AFTERNOON I'VE ENJOYED LESS. WHAT A WASTE. WHAT A DUMB HOBBY.

..OF COURSE, WITH THIS FOR PRACTICE, I'LL BET WE COULD DO GREAT ON ANOTHER MODEL!

LET'S GET ONE OF THOSE CLIPPER SHIPS WITH ALL THE RIGGINGS.

CalViN and HoBBes

by WATTERSON

C'MON, HOBBES. LET ME UP INTO THE TREE FORT.

SAY THE PASSWORD.

NO! YOU KNOW IT'S ME! LET ME UP!

YOU MAY BE SOME OTHER KID IN DISGUISE.

IT'S *ME*, CALVIN! LET ME UP, YOU HAIRBALL BARFER!

AN INSULT! WELL, YOU CAN JUST STAY DOWN THERE *FOREVER*, MR. STINKER.

OH, NO! HERE COMES SUSIE! LET ME UP QUICK, SO WE CAN THROW THINGS AT HER! HURRY! LET DOWN THE ROPE!

LA DE DA DUM DOO ♪♫

SHE'S COMING! QUICK! LET DOWN THE ROPE! I'M SORRY I INSULTED YOU! OK? SEE, I SAID I WAS SORRY! CAN'T YOU LET DOWN THE ROPE?!

YOU HAVE TO SAY THE PASSWORD.

..*Verse Seven*: TIGERS ARE PERFECT, THE *E-PIT-O-ME* OF GOOD LOOKS AND GRACE AND QUIET..UH..UM..DIGNITY..

I WAS GOING TO ASK YOU TO COME OVER AND PLAY HOUSE, BUT I THINK YOU'D BE A WEIRD EXAMPLE FOR OUR CHILDREN.

ONE OF THESE DAYS I'M GOING TO MAKE YOU INTO A RUG! YOU HEAR ME?? A RUG!

CAN I USE THE GARDEN SHOVEL?

WHAT DO YOU WANT IT FOR?

HOBBES AND I ARE GOING ON AN ARCHAEOLOGICAL EXPEDITION.

IF YOU'RE LOOKING FOR FOSSILIZED REMAINS, YOU SHOULD DIG THROUGH YOUR ROOM.

HA HA. SOMEDAY I'LL NAME AN AUSTRALOPITHECUS WOMAN AFTER YOU.

I'VE BEEN READING UP ON PALEONTOLOGY. IT'S AMAZING STUFF.

SCIENTISTS CAN TELL HOW OLD SOMETHING IS JUST BY ANALYZING THE LAYERS OF DIRT IT'S IN.

HEY!

WHY, YOU MUST BE SIX YEARS OLD.

OH, YOU'RE A SCREAM.

ARCHAEOLOGISTS DIG SLOWLY AND CAREFULLY, USING SMALL, DELICATE TOOLS.

EACH ROCK HAS TO BE PAINSTAKINGLY BRUSHED AND SCRAPED SO NOTHING IS BROKEN OR MISSED.

DIG DIG SCRAPE SCRAPE BRUSH BRUSH

ARCHAEOLOGISTS HAVE THE MOST MIND-NUMBING JOB ON THE PLANET.

I DON'T THINK YOUR DAD WILL WANT TO SHAVE WITH THIS TOMORROW.

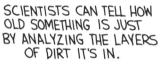

GOSH, LOOK AT ALL THE DINOSAUR BONES WE DISCOVERED.

LET'S GLUE THEM TOGETHER SO WE CAN SEE HOW THEY FIT. THEN YOU CAN DRAW A RECONSTRUCTION OF THE ACTUAL DINOSAUR.

AFTER THAT, WE'LL WRITE UP OUR FINDINGS, AND GET THEM PUBLISHED IN A SCIENTIFIC JOURNAL.

THEN WE'LL WIN THE NOBEL PRIZE, GET RICH, AND GO ON TALK SHOWS.

WHAT ABOUT BABES? WHEN DO WE GET THOSE?

WELL, HERE'S THE COMPLETE SKELETON AS NEAR AS *I* CAN FIGURE OUT.

TRY TO DRAW THE DINOSAUR AS IT REALLY LOOKED WITH MUSCLES AND SKIN.

RIGHT.

WHAT'S IT DOING? WHISTLING?

YOU TELL ME. MAYBE IT'S PUCKERING UP.

SEE THE DINOSAUR SKELETON WE DISCOVERED AND ASSEMBLED?

I'M GOING TO CALL THE NATURAL HISTORY MUSEUM AND TELL THEM THEY CAN HAVE IT FOR TEN BILLION DOLLARS.

THOSE ARE ...UM... PECULIAR BONES.

DO YOU THINK I SHOULD ASK FOR MORE MONEY?

THAT'S NOT *QUITE* WHAT I MEANT.

MOM SAYS SHE DOESN'T THINK WE'VE FOUND A SKELETON AT ALL.

SHE SAYS WE JUST DUG UP SOME TRASH SOMEBODY LITTERED.

OUR DINOSAUR IS A FRAUD.

I GUESS IT WOULDN'T BE RIGHT TO SELL IT TO A MUSEUM THEN.

NOT AT FULL PRICE, ANYWAY.

PSST... SUSIE! CAN I COPY YOUR PAPER?

NO.

CALVIN!

AAAUGHH! I SKINNED MY KNEE! OOH! OW!

AAAUGHHH. OW! OW!

166

Calvin and Hobbes

by WATTERSON

THIS IS CALVIN, YOUR CAPTAIN, SPEAKING...

...JUST TO REASSURE YOU THAT, YES, THERE IS SOMEONE UP FRONT.

CALVIN PILOTS THE JET AIRLINER ACROSS THE COUNTRY AT 35,000 FEET.

HE IS GIVEN CLEARANCE TO LAND. BUT WHAT'S THIS? A PLANE FROM A RIVAL AIRLINE IS MAKING FOR THE SAME RUNWAY TO SHAVE PRECIOUS MINUTES OFF ITS SCHEDULE!

IT'S A 600-MPH GAME OF CHICKEN! CALVIN PULLS BACK ON THE THROTTLE AND LURCHES AHEAD!

THE OTHER PILOT TRIES TO CUT CALVIN OFF WITH A SUDDEN DROP IN ALTITUDE!

CALVIN SWITCHES ON THE "FASTEN SEAT BELT" LIGHT IN THE CABIN, AND DOES A BARREL ROLL!

AT 5 GS, CALVIN HOPES NOT TO BLACK OUT!

AS THEY CLOSE IN ON THE RUNWAY, THE OTHER PILOT HAS NO CHOICE BUT TO PULL UP AND CIRCLE AROUND AGAIN! CALVIN WINS!

HEY, MOM, IS IT TRUE I COULD GET A PILOT'S LICENSE AT AGE 14?

NO.

I HAD NO *IDEA* BINOCULARS WERE SO EXPENSIVE! WE'RE DOOMED! WE'RE DOOMED!

"WE"?

WHY IN THE WORLD DID DAD LET ME USE ANYTHING SO VALUABLE?! HE SHOULD'VE *KNOWN* I'D BREAK THEM! HE MUST'VE BEEN OUT OF HIS MIND! THIS IS ALL *HIS* FAULT!

WHAT AM I GONNA *DO*?

I SUPPOSE YOU *COULD* JUST TELL HIM WHAT HAPPENED...

..AND MAKE MY GETAWAY WHEN THE CORONARY HITS? SAY, *THAT'S* AN IDEA!

MAYBE WE COULD *GLUE* DAD'S BINOCULARS BACK TOGETHER AND HE WOULDN'T EVEN NOTICE! YOU THINK?

IT DEPENDS. WAS THE CASING JUST CHIPPED A LITTLE, OR DID THE LENS ITSELF GET CRACKED?

WELL, MAYBE YOU'D BETTER LOOK AT IT.

DON'T SNEEZE.

MAYBE YOU SHOULD TELL YOUR *MOM* ABOUT THE BINOCULARS, AND SHE CAN HELP SOMEHOW.

TELL MOM?!? ARE YOU CRAZY?? NO WAY!

WHY NOT? YOU'VE GOT TO TELL *SOMEONE*. MAYBE SHE CAN THINK OF SOMETHING.

AT TIMES LIKE THESE, ALL MOM CAN THINK OF IS HOW LONG SHE WAS IN LABOR WITH ME.

LOOK AT DAD, CALMLY EATING HIS DINNER AS IF NOTHING WAS WRONG.

I KNOW HIM. HIS "DAD RADAR" IS BEEPING LIKE CRAZY. HE KNOWS I BROKE *SOMETHING*, HE JUST DOESN'T KNOW *WHAT*. HE CAN'T NAIL ME UNTIL HE KNOWS FOR SURE. HE'LL JUST WAIT. I KNOW HIM.

HE'S GOING TO JUST SIT THERE EATING AND LET ME STEW IN MY OWN GUILT. HE FIGURES SOONER OR LATER I'LL CRACK.

CALVIN?

AAUGH! I DID IT! I DID IT! I'M SORRY! I DIDN'T MEAN TO!!

..PASS THE UH.. ..THE UH...

YOU *BROKE* THE BINOCULARS?!

DIDN'T I TELL YOU TO BE EXTRA, EXTRA CAREFUL WITH THEM?? ISN'T THAT EXACTLY WHAT I SAID?! WELL?!

THOSE BINOCULARS WERE BRAND NEW! HAVE YOU NO RESPECT FOR OTHER PEOPLE'S PROPERTY.?.?.?

I HAVE AN IDEA, DAD. LET'S PRETEND I ALREADY FEEL TERRIBLE ABOUT IT, AND THAT YOU DON'T NEED TO RUB IT IN ANY MORE.

I DIDN'T *MEAN* TO BREAK YOUR BINOCULARS, DAD. IT WAS AN ACCIDENT.

(SNIFF) I'M REALLY SORRY. I FELT LIKE I WAS GOING TO BARF ALL AFTERNOON.

WELL, I'M SORRY I YELLED AT YOU LIKE I DID. I SHOULDN'T HAVE BEEN SO ANGRY.

AFTER ALL, IT WAS JUST A PAIR OF BINOCULARS. IN THE BIG SCHEME OF THINGS, THAT'S REALLY NOT SO BAD.

(SNIFF) REALLY?

SURE. ...IN ANOTHER TEN YEARS, YOU'LL PROBABLY BE WRECKING MY *CAR*.

HOBBES, LOOK! DAD GOT ME MY OWN PAIR OF LITTLE BINOCULARS!

WOW, THESE ARE *YOURS?*

AREN'T THEY GREAT?

I'LL SAY.

DAD SAID AS LONG AS I WAS GOING TO BREAK BINOCULARS, I OUGHT TO AT LEAST BREAK MY OWN.

NOW WE CAN GO TO THE BEACH AND LOOK AT BABES!

MAYBE I SHOULD BREAK DAD'S POWER TOOLS AND SEE IF I COULD GET SOME OF *THOSE.*

WIND WIND WIND

RUMBLE RUMBLE

EITHER I'M GREATLY DECEIVED, OR SOMEONE OPENED A CAN OF TUNA IN THIS VICINITY!

YES... ALL OVER THIS VICINITY.

WHAT A CLEAR NIGHT! LOOK AT ALL THE STARS. MILLIONS OF THEM!

YES, WE'RE JUST TINY SPECS ON A PLANET PARTICLE, HURLING THROUGH THE INFINITE BLACKNESS.

LET'S GO IN AND TURN ON ALL THE LIGHTS.

Calvin and Hobbes by WATTERSON

ZZZZZZZZZZZZ

IS THE BEE STILL ON ME OR NOT?

I'M NOT TELLING. YOU CALLED ME A HAIRBALL.

OK, OK, I'M SORRY. YOU'RE NOT A HAIRBALL. NOW, IS THE BEE THERE OR NOT?

NO.

GOOD. NOW I...

I MEANT "NO, THERE IS A BEE." TODAY IS OPPOSITE DAY!

DON'T FORGET... AT MIDNIGHT OPPOSITE DAY IS OVER, OK?

"YES."

I'M NOT HAVING DINNER TONIGHT.

OH NO?

NOPE. I'M JUST GOING TO EAT COOKIES IN FRONT OF THE TV.

YOU, YOUNG MAN, ARE GOING TO SIT AT THE TABLE AND EAT WHAT I'VE FIXED, JUST LIKE THE REST OF US.

OH, YEAH. THAT'S WHAT I MEANT.

HELLO, I'M WONDERING IF YOU SELL KEGS OF DYNAMITE.

YOU DON'T? HOW ABOUT PLASTIC EXPLOSIVES?

YOU'RE KIDDING. WELL, WHAT ABOUT LAND MINES? DO YOU SELL THOSE? ... YOU DON'T?

LOOK, I'M TRYING TO SEND A GIRL I KNOW INTO DEEP SPACE. PERHAPS YOU COULD SUGGEST SOMETHING.

FWOOOOSH

AS IF LIFE ISN'T SHORT ENOUGH.

WELL, HERE WE ARE! HOME AWAY FROM HOME!

OK, CALVIN, YOU GET OUT WITH YOUR MOM, AND I'LL HAND OUR GEAR TO YOU.

NOW DON'T DROP THIS. IT'S VERY...

OOPS.

PLOONK

DON'T WORRY, DAD. IT'S ONLY ABOUT TEN FEET DEEP. I CAN SEE THE CAMERA AND EVERYTHING.

I AM GOING TO FEED YOU TO THE SEA GULLS, KID.

DEAR, YOU CAME HERE TO *RELAX*.

GOSH, THIS WATER'S COLD! HERE, THAT'S ALL I COULD FIND DOWN THERE. GO GET ME A TOWEL, CALVIN.

IT NEVER FAILS. THE ONE BAG THE KID DUMPS IN THE DRINK HAS ALL THE FRAGILE AND PERISHABLE ITEMS IN IT.

WELL, THE WEEK CAN ONLY IMPROVE FROM HERE.

ONE WOULD LIKE TO *THINK* SO.

HEY, DAD, DID YOU MEAN TO STACK THE TACKLE BOX AND ALL THIS ON YOUR GLASSES?

BOY, DON'T GO NEAR DAD. WHAT A GROUCH!

I DON'T SEE WHY HE CAN'T BE CIVIL JUST BECAUSE I ACCIDENTALLY DROPPED A DUFFEL BAG OVERBOARD AND HE BROKE HIS GLASSES.

ARE YOU GOING TO TELL HIM HE LEFT THE CAR LIGHTS ON BACK WHERE WE GOT THE CANOE?

I THINK *YOU* SHOULD TELL HIM.

184

THERE'S NOTHING TO *DO* HERE.

THAT'S SORT OF THE POINT, DON'T YOU THINK? IT'S GOOD TO STOP RUNNING AROUND.

SOMETIMES ONE SHOULD JUST LOOK AT THINGS AND THINK ABOUT THINGS, WITHOUT *DOING* THINGS.

YOU'RE CERTAINLY THE EXPERT ON *THAT*.

WHAT I LIKE IS WHEN YOU'RE LOOKING AND THINKING AND LOOKING AND THINKING....AND SUDDENLY YOU WAKE UP.

MOM, CAN HOBBES COME IN SWIMMING WITH ME?

I DON'T THINK HE'D BETTER, CALVIN.

WHY NOT?

UM..., TIGERS DON'T SWIM VERY WELL.

THEY DON'T?

FRANKLY, I'M NOT SURE YOUR MOM KNOWS SO MUCH ABOUT TIGERS.

LOOK, WE JUST WANT TO AVOID AN ARGUMENT, RIGHT?

OK, CALVIN, START PACKING UP. WE'RE GOING HOME.

FINALLY!

NOW, NOW. THESE LITTLE OUTINGS ARE VALUABLE EXPERIENCES.

YEAH? HOW?

THEY GIVE US A CHANCE TO BE TOGETHER AS A FAMILY AND LEARN ABOUT OURSELVES.

LIKE HOW WE CAN'T STAND BEING IN SUCH CLOSE PROXIMITY WITH ONE ANOTHER THIS LONG?

EXACTLY.

THIS PROBABLY JUST GOES TO SHOW SOMETHING, BUT I SURE DON'T KNOW WHAT.

THERE'S QUITE A BREEZE UP HERE. I'M REALLY MOVING. THERE'S THE RIVER AND THE TOWN TRIANGLE.

HEY, DOWN THERE! MY NAME IS CALVIN! TELL MY TIGER, HOBBES, I'M BLOWING AWAY ON A BALLOON!

CAN ANYONE HEAR ME? TELL HOBBES HE CAN'T READ MY COMIC BOOKS JUST 'CAUSE I'M NOT AROUND, OK?

...OH, YEAH, TELL MY PARENTS WHAT HAPPENED, TOO, ALL RIGHT? HELLO? HELLO?

UH OH, I'M HEADING INTO A FLOCK OF DUCKS!

EXCUSE ME! COMING THROUGH!

PARDON ME! GANGWAY! BEEP BEEP!

...BOY, IF LOOKS COULD KILL.

MY HANDS ARE GETTING TIRED. I'LL TIE THE BALLOON STRING ONTO MY BELT LOOP.

THERE...

WHOOP

SHOOF

IF A PLANE COMES ALONG NOW, I'M GONNA DIE.

WELL, I SUPPOSE THINGS DON'T GET WORSE THAN HANGING FROM A HELIUM BALLOON A MILE ABOVE SOME UNRECOGNIZED STATE.

OF COURSE, MY GRIP COULD WEAKEN, OR I COULD GET SUCKED INTO A JET INTAKE.

THAT'S ONE OF THE REMARKABLE THINGS ABOUT LIFE. IT'S NEVER SO BAD THAT IT CAN'T GET WORSE.

BOY, I'M JUST GOING HIGHER AND HIGHER.

I SUPPOSE EVENTUALLY THE PRESSURE IN THE BALLOON WILL BE GREATER THAN THE AIR PRESSURE AROUND IT, AND THE BALLOON WILL...

POP!

THIS HAS GOT TO BE A DREAM.

WHENEVER YOU FALL FROM TWO MILES UP IN THE SKY, YOU LOOK DOWN, GASP, AND SUDDENLY WAKE UP.

GASP!

GASP
GASP
GASP
GASP
GASP

I WONDER IF MY LIFE WILL FLASH BEFORE MY EYES.

THAT'S THE PROBLEM WITH BEING SIX YEARS OLD...

...MY LIFE WON'T TAKE VERY LONG TO WATCH.

MAYBE I CAN GET A FEW SLOW-MOTION REPLAYS OF THE TIME I SMACKED SUSIE UPSIDE THE HEAD WITH A SLUSHBALL.

SAY, I WONDER IF I HAVE ANY GUM IN MY POCKET. I COULD BLOW A BIG BUBBLE, AND...

NOPE, NO GUM. LET'S TRY **THIS** POCKET.

MY TRANSMOGRIFIER GUN!!

BOY, THESE THINGS COME IN HANDY ALL THE TIME.

I FORGOT ALL ABOUT MY TRANSMOGRIFIER GUN! NOW I HAVE NOTHING TO WORRY ABOUT!

I'LL JUST POINT IT AT MYSELF AND TRANSMOGRIFY! I'M SAFE!

ZAP

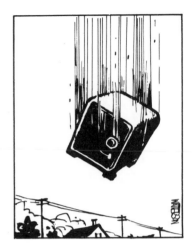

WHERE HAVE YOU BEEN?? I'VE BEEN CALLING AND CALLING. YOUR DINNER'S COLD, I'M SURE.

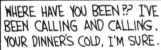

I DRIFTED AWAY ON MY BALLOON AND IT POPPED, BUT FORTUNATELY I HAD MY TRANSMOGRIFIER, SO AFTER I MISTAKENLY TURNED MYSELF INTO A SAFE, I TRANSMOGRIFIED INTO A LIGHT PARTICLE AND ZIPPED BACK HOME INSTANTANEOUSLY!

...OF COURSE, IF I'D KNOWN WE WERE HAVING *THIS*, I WOULDN'T HAVE HURRIED.

SOMETIME YOU SHOULD TRY TRANSMOGRIFYING YOURSELF INTO SOMEONE WHO OCCASIONALLY MAKES AN OUNCE OF SENSE.

CALVIN, I'D LIKE YOU TO PICK UP ALL THE STICKS AND FALLEN BRANCHES IN THE YARD, SO I CAN MOW IT.

WILL YOU PAY ME?

WELL... OK, I'LL PAY YOU A DOLLAR.

A DOLLAR? I WON'T DO IT FOR LESS THAN TWENTY-FIVE!!

IN A MINUTE YOU'LL DO IT FOR NOTHING, JUST BECAUSE I TOLD YOU TO.

...I'LL TAKE THE DOLLAR.

SMART KID.

Calvin and Hobbes
by WATTERSON

SPACEMAN SPIFF EXPLORES THE OUTERMOST REACHES OF THE UNIVERSE.

BY POPULAR REQUEST.

INTREPID EXPLORER SPACEMAN SPIFF LANDS ON AN UNCHARTED PLANET. WHAT STRANGE WONDERS WILL HE DISCOVER HERE?

SPIFF SETS OUT IN SEARCH OF SENTIENT LIFE!

WHAT A STRANGE PLANET THIS IS! ITS SURFACE IS SURPRISINGLY SOFT AND POROUS!

AND HERE CURIOUS GEYSERS BLAST HOT AIR!

SUDDENLY IT DAWNS ON HIM! SPIFF IS NOT ON THE PLANET'S SURFACE AT ALL! HE'S WALKING ON A RECLINING ALIEN!!

OUR HERO SETS HIS DEATH RAY BLASTER.

ZZ.. MMF HM?

LET'S GO, CALVIN! WE'RE ALL READY!

BOY, I HAVEN'T BEEN TO THE ZOO IN AGES. THIS WILL BE FUN.

AND CALVIN'S NEVER BEEN. THIS WILL BE FUN.

I'VE BEEN TELLING HIM ABOUT IT ALL WEEK. HE'S SO EXCITED.

C'MON, CALVIN!

SO WHERE DO WE HAVE TO GO NOW?

BEATS ME. MOM AND DAD ARE ALWAYS DRAGGING US SOME DUMB PLACE.

HOW COME THE ALLIGATORS ARE IN THIS BIG PIT?

SO THEY DON'T GET OUT AND EAT PEOPLE.

DOES THE ZOO EVER THROW ANYONE IN?

DON'T BE SILLY. OF COURSE NOT.

HOW SOON UNTIL WE GO HOME?

LOOK! MONKEYS!

SEE HOW THEY USE THEIR TAILS AND FEET TO CLIMB?

ZOOS LET PEOPLE SEE HOW WILD ANIMALS REALLY BEHAVE.

HEY, LOOK WHAT THAT MONKEY'S DOING! RIGHT IN PUBLIC, TOO! HA HA! THAT'S GROSS! HOW COME I'M NOT ALLOWED TO DO THAT?!

COME LOOK AT THE BIRDS OVER HERE, CALVIN.

WHAT DO YOU THINK OF THE ZOO?

I THINK IT'S KIND OF DEPRESSING.

I ALWAYS FEEL SORRY FOR THE ANIMALS. THEY DON'T HAVE MUCH ROOM TO MOVE, OR ANYTHING TO DO.

THEY JUST SLEEP UNTIL THEY'RE FED.

THAT'S PRETTY MUCH ALL *YOU* DO.

YOU KNOW WHAT I MEAN.

HEY, THOSE KIDS ARE FEEDING THE ANIMALS!

MOM, CAN I GET SOME PEANUTS TO FEED THE ANIMALS?

I'M NOT YOUR MOM.

WHOOP!

ARE YOU LOST? WHAT DOES YOUR MOM LOOK LIKE?

FROM THE KNEES DOWN, SHE LOOKS JUST LIKE YOU.

GOSH, I FOLLOWED THAT LADY HALFWAY AROUND THE ZOO, THINKING SHE WAS MY MOM.

WHY DON'T MOMS WRITE THEIR NAMES ON THEIR CALVES SO THIS KIND OF THING WOULDN'T HAPPEN?

I WONDER WHERE I AM. AND WHERE'S HOBBES? I THOUGHT HE WAS RIGHT WITH ME.

UH OH. WHERE'S CALVIN?

WHY DO THESE LITTLE FAMILY TRIPS ALWAYS TURN OUT THIS WAY? I'M GOING TO SPEND MORE SATURDAYS AT THE OFFICE.

HERE'S HOBBES, BUT WHERE'S CALVIN?

I DON'T SEE HIM.

WHERE COULD HE HAVE GONE? WE JUST TURNED OUR BACKS FOR A MINUTE.

AND WHY DIDN'T HE TAKE HOBBES?

YOU STAY HERE IN CASE HE COMES BACK, AND I'LL GO LOOK FOR HIM.

OK. (SIGH)

BEING A PARENT IS WANTING TO HUG AND STRANGLE YOUR KID AT THE SAME TIME.

SHEESH. CALVIN COULD BE ANYWHERE IN THIS ZOO.

I HOPE HE AT LEAST HAS THE SENSE TO STAY PUT, WHEREVER HE IS.

WHERE WOULD THE LITTLE ROTTER GO IF HE WAS LOST AND SEPARATED FROM HIS STUFFED TOY?

HIS NAME IS HOBBES, AND HE'S... HEY, I'M TALKING TO YOU!!

TIGERS
Panthera tigris

I KNOW! MAYBE CALVIN'S AT THE TIGER PIT, SINCE HE LIKES TIGERS SO MUCH.

HA HA, MAYBE CALVIN'S *IN* THE TIGER PIT, SINCE HE LIKES TIGERS SO MUCH.

YOU FOUND HIM! THANK GOODNESS! WHERE WAS HE?

LOOKING AT THE TIGERS.

I FOLLOWED ANOTHER LADY, THINKING IT WAS MOM, AND THEN WHEN I REALIZED I WAS LOST, I WENT TO ASK THE TIGERS IF THEY'D SEEN HOBBES.

NEXT TIME YOU SHOULD ASK A *PERSON* FOR HELP.

...OH... THAT NEVER OCCURRED TO ME.

ONLY NEXT TIME, THERE WON'T *BE* A NEXT TIME, BECAUSE WE'RE JUST GOING TO TIE YOU TO A STAKE IN THE YARD EVERY WEEKEND.

DEAR!

A FAT LOT OF HELP YOUR COMPATRIOTS WERE, I MIGHT ADD.

DO YOU KNOW WHAT DAY IT IS?

NOPE. WHY?

OH, NO REASON. I WAS JUST CURIOUS.

I SURE LIKE SUMMER VACATION.

SO YOU WANT SOME WATER, HUH? WELL, I'VE GOT A BIG CAN OF IT HERE.

IT'S UP TO *ME* TO DECIDE IF YOU GET WATER OR NOT! *I* CONTROL YOUR FATE! YOUR VERY *LIVES* ARE IN MY HANDS!

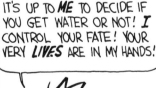

WITHOUT *ME* YOU'RE AS GOOD AS DEAD! WITHOUT *ME*, YOU DON'T...

SAFE!

OK, THAT WAS A SINGLE. I HAVE A GHOST RUNNER HERE NOW, SO I CAN BAT AGAIN.

AND MY GHOST RUNNERS WHO *WERE* ON FIRST AND SECOND BASE ARE NOW ON SECOND AND THIRD, RIGHT?

NOPE. THEY'RE BOTH OUT.

OUT?!

MY GHOST OUTFIELDER TAGGED YOUR GHOST GOING TO THIRD, AND THREW TO MY GHOST SECOND BASEMAN. IT WAS A BRILLIANT DOUBLE PLAY.

THAT NEVER HAPPENED!

YOU'VE GOT TWO OUTS.

WELL, MY GHOST ON FIRST JUST STOLE HOME, SO I'VE GOT ANOTHER RUN! HA HA, SMARTY!

YEAH, WELL, ALL MY OUTFIELD GHOSTS JUST RAN IN AND BEAT THE TOBACCO JUICE OUT OF HIM.

HA! THE GHOST UMPIRE JUST SUSPENDED ALL YOUR GHOSTS FOR ETERNITY. THEY'RE OUT OF THE GAME.

HMPH! IF MY GHOSTS DON'T PLAY, *I* DON'T PLAY.

YOU FORFEIT THE GAME THEN! YOU LOSE AUTOMATICALLY IF YOU QUIT!

THE GHOST CROWD SUPPORTS ME. THEY'RE "BOO"-ING YOU!

SOMETIMES I WISH I LIVED IN A NEIGHBORHOOD WITH MORE KIDS.

BOY, WHAT A BEAUTIFUL SUMMER MORNING, HUH, DAD? TOO BAD YOU CAN'T STAY HOME TO ENJOY IT.

WHEN YOU'RE OLD, YOU'LL BE SORRY YOU NEVER TOOK ADVANTAGE OF DAYS LIKE THESE, BUT OF COURSE, THAT'S FAR OFF, AND IN THE MEANTIME, THERE'S LOTS OF WORK TO BE DONE.

YEP, YOU'D BETTER GO TO WORK. HAVE A GOOD LONG DRIVE IN TRAFFIC. MAYBE YOU'LL GET HOME IN TIME TO WATCH THE SUN SET... IF YOU CAN STAY AWAKE. SO LONG!

GOLLY, I'D HATE TO HAVE A KID LIKE ME.

WHAT WOULD YOU DO IF I CREAMED YOU WITH THIS WATER BALLOON RIGHT NOW?

TAKE THE WORST THING YOU CAN IMAGINE, AND IMAGINE SOMETHING A HUNDRED TIMES WORSE THAN THAT.

YOU'D DO *THAT*?

NO, I'D DO SOMETHING EVEN WORSE.

HE PIQUED MY CURIOSITY.

BIP

WHEEEE.

203

CALVIN and HOBBES by WATTERSON

DINOSAURS EVERYWHERE FLEE FOR THEIR LIVES!

CALVIN IS COMING!

THE LATE CRETACEOUS: THE LAST EPOCH OF THE MIGHTY DINOSAURS!

KING OF THE THUNDER LIZARDS IS THE FEARSOME CALVIN, THE TYRANNOSAURUS!

SEVEN TONS OF MUSCLE AND TEETH. HE SEARCHES FOR PREY!

CALVIN, FOR GOODNESS' SAKE, STOP STOMPING AROUND! YOU'RE DRIVING ME CRAZY!

POW!! CHOMP!

HOW DID THE FEARSOME TYRANNOSAURUS BECOME EXTINCT? NOW WE KNOW!

EVERYTHING FLOATS RANDOMLY IN THE ROOM! THERE'S NO GRAVITY!

CALVIN PUSHES OFF THE CEILING AT A SHARP ANGLE, AIMING FOR THE HALLWAY!

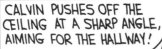

HE GLIDES WITH UNCHECKED MOMENTUM, TURNING HIMSELF TO BE ABLE TO PUSH OFF THE NEXT STATIONARY SURFACE.

C'MON, YOU! OUTSIDE! YOU'RE REALLY BOUNCING OFF THE WALLS TODAY.

AW, MOM.

EXTRA PANTS...

THREE SHIRTS, TWO SWEATERS, TWO SWEATSHIRTS...

ANOTHER PAIR OF PANTS...

STILL TRYING TO LEARN TO RIDE THAT BICYCLE, EH?

I DON'T NEED ANY COMMENTS FROM YOU.

A SHADOW FALLS OVER THE LARGE CITY SKYSCRAPERS!

IT'S A GIGANTIC ANT! WITH ONE FOOTSTEP, IT PULVERIZES THE ENTIRE DOWNTOWN! MILLIONS DIE INSTANTLY!

THE ANT BRUSHES THE CITY OFF THE MAP! PEOPLE FLOOD THE STREETS IN PANIC, ONLY TO BE SMASHED IN THE HORRIBLE WRECKAGE!

WELL... MAYBE I WON'T...

PLANET CALVIN MOVES ACROSS THE SOLAR SYSTEM.

NOBODY NOTICES UNTIL HIS ORBIT TAKES HIM DIRECTLY BETWEEN THE SUN AND EARTH.

CALVIN CAUSES A TOTAL SOLAR ECLIPSE! EARTH IS SHROUDED IN DARKNESS. HOW LONG WILL CALVIN STAY THERE?!

COULD YOU MOVE, PLEASE? YOU'RE IN MY LIGHT.

HA HA HAAA!

ELECTION DAY IS COMING UP. HAVE YOU DECIDED ON A RUNNING MATE?

A RUNNING MATE?

SURE. YOU CAN'T BE ELECTED DAD WITHOUT A MOM, RIGHT?

ARE YOU GOING TO KEEP THE MOM I'VE HAD, OR GET A NEW RUNNING MATE?

GEE...

BEDTIME, CALVIN.

OF COURSE I'LL STICK WITH YOUR MOM.

AWW..

I THINK RITUALS ARE IMPORTANT.

MY FAVORITE RITUAL IS EATING THREE BOWLS OF "CHOCOLATE FROSTED SUGAR BOMBS" AND WATCHING TV CARTOONS ALL SATURDAY MORNING.

AFTER A FEW HOURS, I'M SO OVERSTIMULATED I CAN'T SIT STILL OR EVEN THINK STRAIGHT.

SORT OF A TRANSCENDENTAL EXPERIENCE, HUH?

YEAH. I ACHIEVE A LOWER CONSCIOUSNESS.

218

CalviN aNd HObbEs

by WATTERSON

SCHOOL'S OUT! FREE AT LAST!

AND JUST SIX PRECIOUS HOURS BEFORE BED TO FORGET EVERYTHING I LEARNED TODAY.

I HATE COMING HOME FROM SCHOOL. I NEVER KNOW IF HOBBES IS WAITING TO POUNCE ON ME.

MAYBE I CAN STAND OFF TO THE SIDE HERE, AND PUSH THE DOOR OPEN WITH A STICK.

I'M HOME!

KAPOW!

WHAT DO YOU DO, WAIT UNTIL YOU SEE THE WHITES OF MY EYES?!?

BOY, YOU SHOULD'VE *SEEN* THEM! THEY WERE AS BIG AS DINNER PLATES! HOO HOO HOO!

SO LONG, MOM. HOBBES AND I ARE GOING TO MARS TO LIVE. EARTH IS TOO POLLUTED.

HAVE A GOOD TIME.

SAY GOODBYE TO DAD FOR US. IF I CAN FIND AN INTERPLANETARY POST OFFICE, I'LL WRITE YOU ONCE IN A WHILE AND...

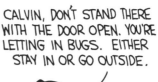

CALVIN, DON'T STAND THERE WITH THE DOOR OPEN. YOU'RE LETTING IN BUGS. EITHER STAY IN OR GO OUTSIDE.

SHE DIDN'T SEEM TOO CHOKED UP ABOUT US GOING, DID SHE?

WE SHOULD'VE LEFT A LONG TIME AGO.

BLAST OFF!

DO YOU REALLY THINK WE'LL GET ENOUGH LIFT TO BREAK EARTH'S GRAVITY?

OF COURSE! YOU THINK I DIDN'T PLAN THIS OUT?! I THOUGHT OF EVERYTHING.

DID YOU THINK OF WHAT YOU'LL EAT ON OUR TRIP?

PACKING WAS *YOUR* JOB! DIDN'T YOU PACK US ANY *FOOD*??

I PACKED FOOD FOR *ME*...

WE DID IT! WE CLEARED EARTH'S ORBIT!

MARS, HERE WE COME!

ARE YOU SURE THIS IS THE WAY?

WHAT? DIDN'T YOU BRING THE MAP?!

SPACE TRAVEL MAKES YOU REALIZE JUST HOW SMALL WE REALLY ARE.

WHEN YOU SEE EARTH AS A TINY BLUE SPECK IN THE INFINITE REACHES OF SPACE, YOU HAVE TO WONDER ABOUT THE MYSTERIES OF CREATION.

SURELY WE'RE ALL PART OF SOME GREAT DESIGN, NO MORE OR LESS IMPORTANT THAN ANYTHING ELSE IN THE UNIVERSE. SURELY EVERYTHING FITS TOGETHER AND HAS A PURPOSE, A REASON FOR BEING. DOESN'T IT MAKE YOU WONDER?

I WONDER WHAT HAPPENS IF YOU THROW UP IN ZERO GRAVITY.

MAYBE YOU SHOULD WONDER WHAT IT'S LIKE TO WALK HOME.

HANG ON! WE'RE COMING IN THROUGH MARS' ATMOSPHERE.

BONK BONK

WE'VE LANDED! WE'RE THE FIRST ONES TO EVER SET FOOT ON ANOTHER PLANET! WHAT A HISTORIC MOMENT!

I STILL CAN'T BELIEVE YOU FORGOT THE CAMERA.

I REMEMBERED IT. *YOU* JUST DIDN'T WANT TO TURN AROUND.

SEE ANY SIGNS OF MARTIAN LIFE?

NOT YET...

HEY, LOOK! IT'S THE OLD "VIKING" SPACECRAFT THAT LANDED HERE IN THE '70s!

GOSH, I WONDER IF IT'S STILL WORKING.

BLAHHHH HOOP HOOP BOOLA ACKACKACK BOOLA

THAT OUGHT TO BLOW SOME CIRCUITS AT NASA!

HEE HEE HEE! I'VE ALWAYS WANTED TO DO SOMETHING LIKE THAT.

WELL, THIS IS OUR NEW HOME. I GUESS WE SHOULD UNPACK AND SET UP CAMP.

COMIC BOOKS... COMIC BOOKS.. TUNA... SOME CANDY BARS... MORE TUNA...TOOTHBRUSHES... A CAN OPENER...LOOKS LIKE WE'RE ALL SET.

WHAT'S THIS?

A NIGHT LIGHT. I THOUGHT IT MIGHT BE SCARY SLEEPING ON A NEW PLANET.

BOY, YOU THOUGHT OF EVERYTHING.

NOW WE HAVE TO FIND AN OUTLET.

YEP, MARS MAY BE A LITTLE DULL, BUT IT'S BETTER THAN EARTH.

CRUNCH CRUNCH

WE'VE GOT A WHOLE PLANET TO OURSELVES. BRAND NEW AND UNSPOILED. NO PEOPLE, NO POLLUTION.

NOTHING BUT RUGGED, NATURAL BEAUTY AS FAR AS THE EYE CAN SEE.

THAT'S NOT YOUR CANDY BAR WRAPPER OVER THERE, IS IT?

IT WAS JUST THERE A MINUTE! *I* WASN'T GOING TO LEAVE IT.

I DON'T KNOW ABOUT YOU, BUT I *LIKE* IT HERE ON MARS.

I DO TOO. IT'S VERY PEACEFUL.

NOT ONLY THAT, BUT WE DON'T HAVE **MOM** HERE TO BOSS US AROUND! NO EARLY BEDTIME, NO BATHS, NO DISGUSTING DINNERS, NO...

DID THAT ROCK JUST MOVE??

MOMMMMM.!!

OH MY GOSH, THAT ROCK MOVED! THERE'S SOMETHING UNDER IT!

IT MUST BE A MARTIAN! OH NO! OH NO! IT'S PROBABLY SOME CREEPY, TENTACLED, BUG-EYED MONSTER!

YOU'RE RIGHT! THERE'S A TENTACLE NOW!

IT'S COMING OUT! WHAT WILL WE DO?!

AAUGHHHH!

IS THE MARTIAN STILL OUT THERE?

I'LL TAKE A PEEK.

I DON'T SEE HIM. HE MUST HAVE HIDDEN.

HIDDEN?? DO YOU THINK HE'S SCARED OF US?

WHY NOT? WE'RE SCARED OF HIM.

YEAH, BUT WE'RE JUST ORDINARY EARTHLINGS, NOT WEIRDOS FROM ANOTHER PLANET, LIKE HE IS.

WHY DO YOU THINK THE MARTIAN HID FROM US?

MAYBE MARTIANS DON'T LIKE EARTHLINGS.

DON'T LIKE US?! WHAT'S NOT TO LIKE?? THERE'S NOTHING WRONG WITH HUMANS!

HEY, YOU MARTIAN! COME ON OUT! WE'RE NOT BAD! WE JUST CAME HERE BECAUSE PEOPLE POLLUTED OUR OWN PLANET SO MUCH THAT...UH.. WHAT I MEAN, IS... UM...

SO WHAT ARE YOU SAYING? THAT OUR REPUTATION PRECEDED US?

WOULD YOU WELCOME IN A DOG THAT WASN'T HOUSE-TRAINED?

HI SUSIE! GUESS WHAT I BROUGHT FOR LUNCH.

NO! GO SIT BY SOMEONE ELSE, OK? YOU ALWAYS SAY YOUR LUNCH IS SOMETHING REVOLTING, AND I DON'T WANT TO HEAR IT!

GEE WHIZ, WHAT'S WRONG WITH YOU? MY LUNCH IS PEANUT BUTTER. WHAT'S SO DISGUSTING ABOUT THAT?!

HMPH. I'M GLAD THAT ONE DAY OUT OF THE YEAR YOU CAN BE CIVIL.

IT'S MY *DESSERT* THAT'S GROSS! LOOK, A THERMOS FULL OF PHLEGM!

CALVIN, WILL YOU RUN AND GET MY PURSE, PLEASE? I NEED THE CALCULATOR.

SURE.

HERE YOU ARE.

THANKS.

AHEM.

I'M NOT GOING TO TIP YOU!!

HUH! SEE IF I EVER FETCH ANYTHING AGAIN.

ELECTION DAY IS COMING UP, DAD. PEOPLE WANT TO KNOW WHERE YOU STAND ON THE ISSUES.

SUCH AS?

LATER BEDTIMES, EXPANDED TV PRIVILEGES, SHORTER SCHOOL WEEKS, AND LESS DISCIPLINE.

I'M AGAINST THEM ALL.

I SEE.

HOW'S YOUR IRA? PRETTY WELL FUNDED?

GO TO BED.

CaLViN and HobbES

by WATTERSON

UH-OH.

SOMETHING IS VERY WRONG HERE.

CALVIN HAS MYSTERIOUSLY SHRUNK TO A QUARTER OF AN INCH TALL!

HOW CAN HE MAKE HIS PLIGHT KNOWN TO HIS PARENTS WHEN HE'S SMALLER THAN A PENNY?

LIBERTY 1977

CALVIN GETS AN IDEA! HE GRABS THE LEG OF OF A PASSING HOUSEFLY AND FLIES TO HIS DAD'S CAMERA!

ONCE THERE, HE CLIMBS UP AND SETS THE SELF-TIMER.

SE TI

JUMPING ON THE SHUTTER, CALVIN HAS FIFTEEN SHORT SECONDS TO GET IN FRONT OF THE LENS!

WATTERSON

WITH LUCK, CALVIN'S DAD WILL HAVE THE FILM DEVELOPED SOON, AND DISCOVER WHAT HAS HAPPENED!

WHAT HAPPENED?! LOOK AT ALL THESE TERRIBLE PICTURES! I DON'T REMEMBER TAKING THESE. WHO'S THAT LITTLE SPECK IN THE DISTANCE ALL THE TIME? YOU HAVEN'T BEEN FOOLING WITH MY CAMERA, HAVE YOU?

ME? HECK, NO. MAYBE YOU SHOULD GET THE CAMERA FIXED.

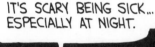

WELL, IT LOOKS LIKE CALVIN JUST CAUGHT THE BUG GOING AROUND. NOTHING SERIOUS.

KEEP AN EYE ON HIM, AND LET ME KNOW IF HE ISN'T FEELING BETTER SOON.

OK. THANK YOU.

SO LONG, CALVIN. YOU WERE A GOOD PATIENT THIS TIME.

MM.

NOTHING LIKE A LITTLE VIRUS TO TAKE THE EDGE OFF A KID.

I'D STILL RATHER LET HIS TEACHER DEAL WITH HIM.

I GET TO STAY HOME FROM SCHOOL TODAY.

I GET TO LIE IN BED, DRINK TEA, AND READ COMIC BOOKS ALL DAY.

I WISH I COULD DO THIS EVERY DAY.

... LIKE SOME PEOPLE I KNOW.

YOUR MOM DOESN'T BRING *ME* TEA IN BED.

I WANT SOME MORE TOAST.

ROOM SERVICE!!

HA! *THAT* SURE GOT YOU UP HERE QUICK!

TOMORROW YOU'RE GOING TO SCHOOL.

I THINK PEOPLE WORRY TOO MUCH ABOUT LITTLE THINGS.

ALL THEY DO IS MAKE THEMSELVES UNHAPPY THAT WAY.

WHY GET AN ULCER OVER THINGS THAT DON'T REALLY MATTER?

LIKE THE BOOK REPORT YOU'RE SUPPOSED TO BE WRITING NOW ON THE BOOK YOU HAVEN'T READ?

EXACTLY. CASE IN POINT.

WHY IN THE WORLD AM I WAITING IN THE POURING RAIN FOR THE SCHOOL BUS TO TAKE ME SOMEWHERE I DON'T EVEN WANT TO GO?

I GO TO SCHOOL, BUT I NEVER LEARN WHAT I WANT TO KNOW.

I HATE SCHOOL.

EACH DAY I COUNT THE HOURS UNTIL SCHOOL'S OVER. THEN I COUNT THE DAYS UNTIL THE WEEKEND. THEN I COUNT THE WEEKS UNTIL THE MONTH IS OVER, AND THEN THE MONTHS UNTIL SUMMER.

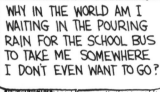

I ALWAYS HAVE TO POSTPONE WHAT I *WANT* TO DO FOR WHAT I *HAVE* TO DO!

WELCOME TO THE WORLD.

WOULD YOU SIGN THIS PARENTAL EXCUSE TO GET ME OUT OF THE NEXT 11½ YEARS OF SCHOOL?

Calvin and Hobbes

by WATTERSON

THE VALIANT SPACEMAN SPIFF, INTERGALACTIC EXPLORER, COMES IN OVER THE MOUNTAINS OF A STRANGE PLANET!

OUR HERO DESPERATELY HOPES TO FIND A REST AREA WITH WORKING FACILITIES.

SPACEMAN SPIFF LANDS ON THE DISTANT PLANET ZOKK!

CLIMBING DOWN FROM HIS SPACECRAFT, OUR HERO PREPARES TO EXPLORE THE SURFACE!

UNEXPECTEDLY, SPIFF'S FIRST STEP SENDS HIM CAREENING THROUGH THE SKY!

SPIFF QUICKLY REALIZES THAT PLANET ZOKK HAS ONLY A FRACTION OF EARTH'S GRAVITY!

OOF

WITH PRACTICE, OUR HERO SOON FINDS HE CAN BOUND EFFORTLESSLY ACROSS THE LANDSCAPE!

WATTERSON

STOP BOUNCING ON THE BED AND GO TO SLEEP!

DUMB BALLOON.

POOF POOF

POOF POOOF

POOFF

HEY, SUSIE, DID YOU HAVE ANY TROUBLE WITH OUR MATH HOMEWORK LAST NIGHT?

NO, WHY?

I THOUGHT A COUPLE OF THESE WERE TRICKY. CAN I CHECK MY ANSWERS WITH YOURS?

OK.

THANKS. WHAT DID YOU GET FOR QUESTION ONE?

SEVEN.

SEVEN? GOOD, THAT'S WHAT I GOT. WHAT DID YOU GET FOR QUESTION TWO?

DROP DEAD, CALVIN.

EVER SIT AND WATCH ANTS?

LOOK AT THIS ONE. HE'S CARRYING A CRUMB THAT'S BIGGER THAN HE IS, AND HE'S *RUNNING*.

AND IF YOU PUT AN OBSTACLE IN FRONT OF HIM, HE'LL SCRAMBLE LIKE CRAZY UNTIL HE GETS ACROSS IT. HE DOESN'T LET ANYTHING STOP HIM.

I JUST CAN'T IDENTIFY WITH THAT KIND OF WORK ETHIC.

Calvin and Hobbes

by WATTERSON

WELL DAD, WE'RE RIGHT DOWN TO THE WIRE, AND THE POLLS SAY YOU WON'T BE DAD HERE MUCH LONGER.

IT SEEMS YOU'RE JUST NOT LIKEABLE ENOUGH. THOSE POLLED CONTINUE TO FIND YOU A COLD FISH.

IF YOU WANT SOME ADVICE, I'D SUGGEST YOU DO SOMETHING EXTRAORDINARILY LIKEABLE IN THE NEXT TWO MINUTES.

GO TO BED.

NO, NO! IT'S *WAY* TOO LATE TO LEARN HOW TO TELL JOKES.

TEN... FIFTEEN... SIX... TWENTY-TWO...

HIKE!

YAAA... AUGH!

ANOTHER FIVE YARD LOSS!

WE'VE GOT TO GET SOME OTHER PLAYERS.

BOY, YOU'RE LUCKY *YOU* DON'T HAVE TO GO TO SCHOOL LIKE *I* DO.

YOU DON'T KNOW WHAT IT'S LIKE TO GET UP ON THESE COLD, DARK MORNINGS AND HAVE TO GO SOMEPLACE YOU HATE.

YES I DO.

OH YEAH? HOW COULD YOU?

YOU TELL ME EVERY MORNING.

OH, AM I KEEPING YOU AWAKE?! I'M *SORRY!*

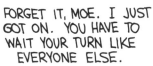

CALVIN and HOBBES

by WATERSON

RINGGG

WHAT A DAY.

YOU THINK THAT'S FUNNY? COME BACK AND FIGHT, YOU WEASEL!

WHAT HAPPENED TO *YOU*??

DON'T ASK. I'M GOING UPSTAIRS TO CHANGE.

CALVIN'S ROOM
• ENTER & DIE •

NOT AGAAINN!

WHERE'S CALVIN?

I SENT HIM TO HIS ROOM. I CAUGHT HIM MAKING PRANK CALLS TO PET STORES, ASKING IF THEY'D BUY HIS TIGER.

WHEN I GROW UP, I WANT TO BE AN INVENTOR. FIRST I WILL INVENT A TIME MACHINE.

THEN I'LL COME BACK TO YESTERDAY

AND TAKE MYSELF TO TOMORROW

AND SKIP THIS DUMB ASSIGNMENT.

MOMMM, I'M HOME FROM SCHOOL! OPEN THE DOOR FOR ME, OK?

WHAT'S THE MATTER? IT WASN'T LOCKED.

SOMETIMES HOBBES IS WAITING TO POUNCE ON ME AS SOON AS I OPEN THE DOOR.

OH FOR HEAVEN'S SAKE! FROM NOW ON, DON'T CALL ME TO COME TO THE DOOR UNLESS IT'S LOCKED.

HA! I SURE OUT-SMARTED HOBBES *THIS* TIME!

THBBPTT!

SISSY.

BOY, I'M IN A BAD MOOD TODAY! EVERYONE HAD BETTER STEER CLEAR OF ME!

I HATE *EVERYBODY!* AS FAR AS I'M CONCERNED, EVERYONE ON THE PLANET CAN JUST DROP DEAD. PEOPLE ARE SCUM.

WELL-L-L? DOESN'T ANYONE WANT TO CHEER ME UP?!?

The·End